THE LIMITS OF HOUSING POLICY

PETER KING

THE LIMITS OF HOUSING POLICY

A Philosophical Investigation

MIDDLESEX UNIVERSITY PRESS

First published in 1996 by
Middlesex University Press

Middlesex University Press is an imprint of
Middlesex University Services Limited,
Bounds Green Road, London N11 2NQ

A CIP catalogue record for this book is available from
The British Library

ISBN 1 898253 09 9

Typeset in Times 11/14pt from the author's disk by
Scriptmate Editions
Manufacture coordinated in UK by
Book-in-Hand Ltd London N6 5AH

ACKNOWLEDGEMENTS

I have many people to thank for their help and assistance throughout the writing of this book. It began as early as 1988 when I registered as a part time PhD student at the University of Bradford with the aim of exploring the politics behind the *Housing Act 1988*. My interest soon shifted to a more overtly philosophical consideration of housing whilst still using the 1988 reforms as the point of departure. As the research developed the philosophy took over and I am extremely thankful that in Mich Le Lohe I had a supervisor of such experience, confidence and wisdom. If he ever had any doubts about the direction in which I was going he never showed it, nor did he attempt to dissuade me from travelling along the particular idiosyncratic route that has led to this work.

I completed my PhD thesis, titled *Modern Conservatism, Liberal Ironism and the Significance of Housing* in July 1993. Since then the work has developed considerably and I am grateful to a number of people for their criticism and comments. Firstly, I am grateful to my two PhD examiners, Johnston Birchall from Brunel University and Alan Carling from Bradford. Their comments and criticisms were particularly useful in the redrafting of the book into what I hope is a more cohesive format. Also I appreciate their acceptance and encouragement of what was an untypical work of housing research.

I have also benefited from the comments, criticisms and continued dialogue with my colleagues at the Centre for Comparative Housing Research at De Montfort University, Leicester. In particular I am grateful to Mike Oxley for commenting on an earlier draft of the book which helped me to firm up its focus. Also I have benefited from discussions with Tim Brown, Richard Tomlins and Andrew Golland. I also thank those students who have had responded to parts of this book delivered on various BSc and MSc modules over the last three years — the opportunity to defend one's ideas and position is always instructive even if it is sometimes a disabusing one.

In the latter stages of preparation I am grateful to various people connected with Middlesex University Press. In particular Tim Putnam has offered detailed and helpful comments on several drafts. I am also grateful to the anonymous reviewers who have commented on the work in its various stages.

I would also like to thank Jim Kemeny for his comments on Chapter One. I am afraid that I have not had the opportunity to respond fully to them. I therefore beg his forgiveness for presenting our respective positions as perhaps being further apart than they infact are. As I hope I make clear in Chapter One, my criticism of Jim's work derives not from a lack of respect, but from an appreciation that it is a groundbreaking attempt to widen housing discourse. Indeed this essay could not have been written without something as significant as *Housing and Social Theory* to react against.

I am indebted to my brother, Graham, who guided me through the fearful complexities of the personal computer and prepared the original idea for the cover design of this book. He showed great restraint in continually turning down the opportunity of patronising his elder brother.

Finally, I turn to those people to whom this book is dedicated. Since starting this book I have got married and become the father of two daughters. Indeed the birth of our daughter, Helen, in April 1993 was the incentive to finally complete my PhD . Since then I have carried on working on this project and I am grateful for the patience shown by Barbara in putting up with the selfishness of writing. I also beg forgiveness from Helen and Rachel for turning down their requests for stories and games. I fear that they already know it will happen again!

We are, perhaps inevitably, not as original and innovative as we think we are and I must therefore, right at the start, pay my intellectual debts. As a work of *critique* rather than empirical research this essay has been formed through reading and thinking about the work of others. In particular its development can be traced from the reading of just one book, *Housing by People* by John Turner. This jaunt into 'the philosophy of housing' was sparked off by Colin Ward's description of John Turner as 'something much rarer than a housing expert: he is a philosopher of housing, seeking answers to questions which are so fundamental that they seldom get asked' in the preface to Turner's book (1976, p. 4). Whilst I don't pretend to be asking questions as fundamental as those asked by Turner, the very notion of a philosophy of housing was one I found inspiring. As will be apparent from even a cursory reading of what follows I have learnt much from reading John Turner's little book and I still turn to it again and again to remind myself what is important in the housing process and what values *should* matter.

This is not, however, a philosophy of housing in any comprehensive sense. I have rather sought to use philosophical ideas and descriptions in order to illuminate the process of housing. My aim was to get beyond the typical analyses of housing which stress production and consumption issues (or how policy is implemented in order to control production and consumption). These discourses see the housing process as a concern for physical entities. Once the issue of access has been discussed and decided upon, little attention is paid to what households might wish to do with the physical entity they have acquired or been allocated. In short the typical analysis of housing portrays housing *as an end in itself*.

The basic premise behind this essay is that housing is not itself an end but a *means* whereby households may fulfil their own ends. The physical entity we call the dwelling has significance because of what a household is able to do in it. Thus the amenities provided by the dwelling are not important in themselves, but because they facilitate the achievement of the particular aims of the household. In this light housing is more usefully seen not use as a collection of physical entities but also as a process. As Turner famously stated, housing is both a noun and a verb.

In developing this basic premise I made three important assumptions which I state here without attempting to justify them. Firstly, it is assumed that housing is an individual process. Whilst we often talk of public or social housing, we live privately not publicly or socially. The primary experience of housing is as individuals in households, not as a community. I am not trying to deny the notions of community or society, but rather to make it clear that communities are made up primarily of individuals and that societal change occurs because of the actions of individuals.

Secondly, I have tried to show that it is not merely actions themselves that are important, but the perceptions of these actions. This concern for perception follows on from the notion that housing is a means and not an end in itself. It is not what housing is but how it is perceived because what matters is how we use it and react to it as individuals. Perception is also important in the description of public policy which forms much of Part One of this essay. I seek to show that it is not what happens or is intended that determines change, but the perception of actions and intentions. This has several important implications. Firstly, it places the emphasis back on the individuals who 'receive' the outcomes of public policy. Secondly, it adds to the complexity of policy making by suggesting that these outcomes are in part determined by the perception of the 'receivers'. This complexity should not be understated, because unlike the superficially similar notion of rational expectations, I do not suggest that perceptions are rational or predictable. The third implication of the importance of perception is that if the mixing of individual perceptions create such complexity then perhaps we should question the whole notion of public policy making as it is currently envisaged. As the title of this essay shows, this last implication is at the centre of these descriptions.

The final assumption which I drew on is that there is no foundation on which individual action can be grounded other than their perception. There is no underpinning epistemological framework on which individuals can draw on to support their moral position. My position is thus both pragmatic and relativist.

This essay, by adopting an individualist and antirealist position, will find little favour with many housing researchers and commentators. It is not, however, my intention to adopt a deliberately controversial position. I believe that my position is a serious and a substantive one which is worthy of discussion within the mainstream of housing and social policy discourse. However, I am not attempting to prove that my position is better than any others — I leave that to those who insist on universalism — but rather to add to what I see as a developing conversation between those interested in housing and social policy. I am not seeking to persuade, but only to interest and engage others who think and write in this field. Moreover I do not even claim that the following descriptions are 'right', merely possible, and in the normative sense, desirable.

Indeed I have not sought to hide the normative elements within the following descriptions. To insist on an academic objectivity whilst presenting a relativist position would be absurd. However, if I may say so, the only difference between this position and that of apparently objective universalism is one of honesty.

This essay is particularly critical of modernity. I suggest that current housing policy is an example of modernity's desire for progress and uniformity. It fails precisely because these universalist tendencies are inconsistent with the incommensurable desires and interests of individuals. I am, however, reluctant to suggest that this is a postmodern work. This is not because I wish to disassociate myself from many of the ideas and writers who are so labelled, but rather because I see the term as increasingly being associated with formulaic responses based on an unreflective acceptance of writers such as Derrida, Foucault and Lyotard . The term is thus fast falling into disrepute. This, I would suggest, is unfortunate because there is much that is original and significant in these writers and others such as Rorty and Levinas. I have thus made use of these writers when I have felt they can offer an insight into the problems of modernity and its possible alternatives. But I have also chosen to combine these writers with others such as Berlin and Nozick who can at least nominally be claimed by the modernist tradition.

Thus whilst this may not be the most original work on housing, I would like to think that it is different and distinctive. This is not, I hope, gratuitous, but because housing policy is in need of rethinking. This can only be achieved if the way we think, talk and write about housing is rethought. This is a modest attempt to do just that.

Peter King
Peterborough
August 1996

To Barbara, Helen and Rachel

'the chief part of human happiness arises
from the consciousness of being beloved'

Adam Smith, *The Theory of Moral Sentiments*

Contents

INTRODUCTION   15

Part One: The Problem with Housing

THE SIGNIFICANCE OF HOUSING   33

MODERNIST HOUSING POLICY   59

THE FAILURE OF MODERNIST HOUSING POLICY   98

Part Two: The Need for Limits

PLURALISM AND ANTI-ESSENTIALISM   121

AUTONOMY, RIGHTS AND HOUSING NEED   139

A VERNACULAR HOUSING PROCESS   159

Part Three: The Limits of Housing Policy

A FRAMEWORK FOR POLICY   185

CONCLUSION   194

BIBLIOGRAPHY   201

INDEX   209

INTRODUCTION

Despite the jargon of modern housing discourse, which designates housing according to its means of provision (public, private, social, etc.) housing only has a meaning because of its use. Use, real or perceived, of course, does not necessarily alter with the type of provision. It depends rather on the nature and circumstances of the particular household in the particular dwelling. However, I do not intend to present merely another discourse in favour of perceiving housing in terms of consumption instead of provision, but is rather a call to see housing — as product and consumable — in terms of perception itself.

It is my intention to show that the significance of housing — and hence its value — is derived out of how households perceive the relation between themselves and their housing as parts of a dynamic environment. Households are thus to be seen as implicated within any framework that attempts to determine the significance of housing. It is the household as a primary organised and organising unit that defines the appropriate use and therefore the consequent significance of housing, both in terms of production and consumption. This is because housing is not a mere commodity or unit with a material value. The definition of housing that will be developed in this essay will stress other values than the material or economic, and hence I shall tend to use the term *dwelling* to connote a more inclusive and encompassing, yet necessarily vaguer process concept. Dwelling will be equated to the action of doing — dwelling is something one does — rather than having. I am therefore not restricting myself to a discourse about commodities and access to them. I can demonstrate this opening up of discourse by examining the values that may be attached to housing in the policy process.

Housing policy, like most if not all government initiatives, seeks to create a series of expectations within households in order to obtain a particular effect. In the case of the Conservative governments after

1979, policy has been aimed at shifting expectations towards the viability of ownership for the majority of households. This has been achieved through the continued subsidisation of mortgage finance, the offering of discounts for council tenants to purchase their property alongside a policy of massive expenditure cuts to public housing providers, and a hostile rhetoric aimed at marginalising and denigrating local authorities as landlords (Cole and Furbey, 1994; Hills, 1991; Malpass, 1990; Malpass and Murie, 1994). The aim of policy was to link housing to property within a market. This was intended to serve the economic, political and moral purposes of the Modern Conservative ideal.

However, the reality of this policy has been inconsistent with its intentions. It created a particular series of expectations and these have not been realised. The reason for this was that housing policy became inextricably linked into the larger economic and political considerations of government. Expectations were based upon housing as a wealth creator — as an investment good whose performance in a deregulated market has become significant as an economic indicator. Thus housing has become a good in a speculative market and accordingly, a legitimate lever for Government action on the economy. The political significance of housing for the Modern Conservatives is as a form of economic property accessible to the majority.

But ownership achieves nothing of itself. A market value is relevant only if a stable market exists. If one cannot sell a house, can it still be said to have an exchange value in anything but a purely hypothetical sense? It could be said that alternatively a house's value may lie in its collateral value. A house may be used as security for borrowing whether it can be sold immediately or not. However, this begs the question of affordability in a market where exchange value is divorced from cost. Unstable markets are characterised by unstable prices, and this has been graphically demonstrated by both the prices of consumption and exchange in the British owner-occupied market since the mid-1980s. If one is unable to afford the immediate costs of consumption, and one has no certainty of the stability of these costs over time, then the collateral potential of one's house is an irrelevance. Indeed one's priorities are likely to be towards reducing one's debt rather than adding to it.

Thus, whilst housing can be seen as an asset, it should equally be shown in the debit side of the household balance sheet as a liability. What differs over time is the immediacy of housing as an asset or as a liability.

This policy failure, however, is not restricted to the post-1979 period. Indeed the policies introduced by the Thatcher and Major Governments were promulgated as responses and remedies to the policy failures of the period 1945–1979. Regardless of the ideological import of the Modern Conservative critique of social democracy, the failures of the post-war period were palpable. Power (1987) has shown that the dominant emphasis in public housing development in Britain has been on *property rather than people*. This emphasis on property creates an immediate link to the succeeding period, for we shall see that property rights are a defining characteristic of the Modern Conservatives. However, Power is using the term "property" here to define the built form as opposed to the rights over it. She is using the term in its *common sense* meaning rather the *philosophical* sense (MacPherson, 1978). But this does not negate the connection between the two periods as both conceptions are totalising abstractions that serve to determine the dwelling environment. The effects of these policies thus show a degree of similarity.

Housing policy in the period of mass council housebuilding concentrated on the development rather than the management of rented housing. This development was carried out on a large scale in the "strong belief that housing had to be produced on a massive scale to combat poor conditions and house a growing population" (Power, 1987, p. xiv).

The policy was dictated by particular perceptions of apparent housing needs as dictated by a process of planning. The needs, as determined by centralised planning techniques, indicated that what was needed was development on a massive scale.

This situation was compounded by "the almost exclusive reliance on councils as direct landlords" (Power, 1987, p. xiv). This combination of large scale provision and a virtual monopoly of the process by one sector was, according to Power, "out of all proportion to the management skills or community needs of local areas" (p. ix). This arose out of the Attlee Government's determination to make council housing if not a universal then certainly a general service like health and education. The aim was to create a service for all, rather than just for the poorest and the worst housed. Indicative of this was the measure within the Housing Act 1949 to remove the statutory restriction limiting council housing to 'the working classes'. Council housing was thus seen as the total solution to the post war housing crisis.

The difficulty of this approach, however, is that whilst health care and education are essentially merit goods, housing maintains its existential quality regardless of one's condition and place in the lifecycle. Our demand for housing is thus a permanent one and the total demand within a community will thus remain high (what alters is the degree of the latency of demand, or, as I shall suggest, the level of the fulfilment of need). When this is allied to the major logistical, political and financial difficulties in providing large scale housing the potential for the dislocation of policy is great.

Power identified the two main problems of this policy as being, firstly, the time lags involved in slum clearance and the resulting redevelopment, and secondly, the mismatch between the provision of housing and the desires of the presumed residents.

Slum clearance was the necessary precursor of any future redevelopment. The immediate consequence of the clearance programme was to create an acute local housing shortage as the houses were demolished. However, by the time that these houses had been replaced by more modern developments — often a period of several years — many of the former residents had moved away to alternative accommodation. Thus the effect of time lags was to lead to a reduction in local housing demand, depopulation of the inner cities and the scattering of long standing communities. As Power remarks, "(t)he most significant element in slum clearance was the dispersal that it caused of settled urban neighbourhoods" (1987, p. 53).

This leads to the second main problem of the policy of mass centralised provision. The concentration on council provision was at odds with the desires of many of the intended beneficiaries. The post war council house building programme coincided with a major increase in owner occupation. The policy of mass provision based on apparent housing need coincided with a period of increasing affluence with the consequent ability of increasing numbers of households to provide for themselves. Therefore, whilst the main thrust of national policy was to provide housing for all sections of the community many households aspired to a different tenure. The consequence of this situation was a mismatch between supply and demand as "(c)ouncils acted though they were building for infinite demand. Yet the very rapid expansion owner-occupation since the war infact constantly eroded demand" (Power, 1987, p. 58).

The policy led to a mismatch in a further way, in that a considerable amount of the housing produced has proven to be unpopular. This is because, as critics such as Birchall (1988), Turner (1972; 1976), and Ward (1985; 1990) have suggested, centralised policy has dictated the particular types of dwellings without due regard to the desires of the users. Indeed, central policy making is incapable of matching provision with desires because of the level of aggregation required for this level of policy formulation.

In Britain much of this unpopular housing is in the form of high rise and high density estates. This form of development was encouraged through the subsidy system which between 1956 and 1961 offered local authorities up to 300% higher subsidy for building over five storeys high (Power, 1987). These estates proved to be unpopular not so much because of their level of amenity, but rather because of the dispiriting and alien environment they created in contrast to the conventional low rise street developments of the so called "slums", which, for all their lack of modern amenities, met with the perceptions of the dwellers in terms of their referencing to family, community and locality. The issue could thus be portrayed as one of understandability of the dwelling process and the consequent environment.

The implementation of British housing policy, as this example demonstrates, is a top down approach with resources and regulation percolating downwards according to criteria decided at the top. This discussion has centred upon the British experience, yet there are examples of this form of totalising provision in the USA (Jacobs, 1961), Latin America (Turner and Fichter, 1972; Turner, 1976) and Africa (Uduku, 1994). Indeed housing, in Britain and elsewhere, is a particularly graphic example of the universalising and globalising tendencies of modernity.

Modernity can be seen as the attempt to develop an objective science and a universality morality and law. These were to be autonomous systems of thought in the sense of operating according to their own inner logic rather than being circumscribed by external pressures (Harvey, 1989). It involved the belief that a better world could be constructed through the active pursuit of rationality, objectivity and a common morality. Thus humanity is portrayed as progressing towards a particular purpose which is necessarily universal as it is deemed to lead to an improvement in the human condition. According to Harvey (1989), modernity "took it as axiomatic that there was only one possible answer to any question" (p. 27).

The significance of this universalism for housing policy can be demonstrated in the writings and influence of Le Corbusier (1927, 1929). He believed that the world had moved to a new age of industrialisation and mass consumption. He therefore takes the American factory as his model with its emphasis of function over form and its uniform, regular patterned aesthetic. Consistent with this industrial ethic, Le Corbusier perceived the need for "the mass-production house, healthy (and morally so too) and beautiful in the same way that working tools and instruments which accompany our existence are beautiful" (1927, p. 27).

As he famously stated, a house is "a machine for living in" (1927, p. 4). Thus the house has a particular function, and its beauty is derived from this functionality. These industrialised methods are applicable because "all men have the same needs" (1927, p. 136) which may be met by the application of standards. These standards serve to "put order into human effort" (1927, p. 135). Thus Le Corbusier's industrial ethic can be imposed upon human activity through the creation of a disciplined environment. The standardisation called for by Le Corbusier "demands" (1929, p. 76) uniformity both in housebuilding and in town planning. This is because "(t)he house, the street, the town are points to which human energy is directed: they should be ordered, otherwise they counteract the fundamental principles around which we revolve" (1929, p. 15).

The implication behind Le Corbusier's aesthetic is that these "fundamental principles" are universal and therefore applicable everywhere that humanity is. His industrial aesthetic is conceived as *the* solution to the modern "problem" of housing. The influence of this aesthetic has been considerable as I have shown with the discussion of the mass council house building in the post war period. The belief that there was one means of solving the post war housing shortage could be attributed to modernity's universalism, of which Le Corbusier is a particularly pertinent example.

One of the consequences of the universalising tendency within modernity has been to assert the inevitability of what are in fact arbitrary and contingent processes — there is no grounding for placing an industrial ethic above any other, except that it became fashionable and ultimately accepted. The grail of progress is suggested as leading humanity towards a particular series of outcomes which are readable through a number of metanarratives (Lyotard, 1984). These metanarratives are consequently stated as categoricals and are given the status of objective certainties through their claims of universality. What this implies is a commitment towards the metanarrative as the objective determinant of progress itself. It is this commitment that allows the metanarratives of modernity the space to create and recreate reality through the manipulation of perception and the consequent significance attributed to objects, movements and ideas. These implications suggest that the role of ideology plays a prominent role in the creation and development of modernist forms of provision.

It is the role of ideology that will be seen as a principal determinant in the formation of the totalising forms of provision seen in post war Britain. The description of Modern Conservative ideology will form a significant part of the early part of this essay. It will be contended that it is the very facets of a modernist ideology has led to the failure of policies predicated upon it.

However, in response to this ideology of modernity I shall present a description of dwelling where human values supplant market values. This does not negate the issue of the affordability of housing, but adds to it issues such as the control of the housing process and its proximity to family and employment in the determination of adequate and stable housing. Housing that allows households freedom of action and to maintain their links with family and to minimise their transport and commuting costs have been shown to be of primary significance to households across the world (Skinner and Roddell, 1983; Turner and Fichter, 1972; Turner, 1976).

An emphasis on housing as property forgets what is an important role for housing, as a place of security and enabling for a household. This is to realise the significance of human values rather than the monetary value of housing. However to talk of human values in the abstract is to miss the point of their significance. A discussion has to be conducted in a way that does not seek to generalise. The significance of human values is that they are *personal* — they are what individuals think and feel. The important distinction is that human values are dictated by the household, whilst monetary value is determined by the asset they reside in and its attractiveness within a market. Thus a concern for human values concentrates on the process of housing rather than the house itself, but in a way that is non-totalising and personalising.

Of course such a description can only be partial. It must restrain itself to concentrating on the processes that help to determine dwelling rather than what dwelling itself should be like. Indeed my critique of the Modern Conservative vision will make much of its totalising tendencies, and thus I shall take particular concern to avoid it myself when presenting an alternative.

The significance of such an approach can be shown by contrasting housing as a noun and as a verb — 'a house' as opposed to 'to house' (Turner, 1972; 1976). Housing can be seen as the physical structures in which people dwell. It is equipment that provides shelter, "a machine for living in" (Le Corbusier, 1927). It is a concern for standards of amenity, for space standards and overcrowding. It is where homelessness is seen simply as a deficit of housing rather than a deficit in autonomy and security. According to this perception, housing is merely a material aggregation that poses certain technical and managerial questions for professionals to solve. This view is what leads to a preoccupation with provision in prescribed ways that I see as being at the centre of national housing policy.

However, to see housing as a verb is for it to become a process. It is the process of providing shelter *and* of living in and with the results. It takes the conception of housing beyond the material towards a concern with the meanings human beings find in shelter (Norberg-Schulz, 1985). Instead of a concern with what housing is, it is preoccupied with an exploration of what housing does. The emphasis on housing as a process does not necessarily imply self-building, although this is an option (and indeed a necessity for many, particularly in the Third World). Rather it begs the questions of what autonomy can be exercised by the dwellers and consequently what level of control they can expect. It is not a concern for prescribing the involvement within processes, but rather who controls the very processes themselves.

Housing when used either as a noun and a verb relates to both quality and quantity, but the approaches are radically different. The preoccupation with physical structure tends to lead to a determination of quality in terms of generalised standards, and quantity in terms of units of accommodation. Such a concern has given us building and planning regulations, an apparent obsession with annual housing starts and housing need defined in terms of the number of dwellings needed per year.

The process based concept, however, is concerned with the relative notion of fulfilment, and thus not with generalised standards. What is sufficient in terms of the quality and quantity of a dwelling is for the individual household to decide. This notion, because it is a relative one, personalises housing. It is a view that relegates the significance of aggregated physical structures and standards and places over it an analysis that is necessarily subjective. This subjectivity is because the analysis concentrates on the households who inhabit the structures and not on supposedly objective and rational economic players. It is thus a personalised view of housing — on what it does in people's lives.

Stressing this view, however is not to deny the physicality of housing. The process involves the creation of shelter, and it sees this as a physical as well as a cultural and personally defining space. But the building and provision of shelter is not an end in itself. Shelter is necessary only as a tool for the fulfilment of personal needs. Appropriate, adequate, good quality shelter is the starting point, rather than being the purpose itself. Shelter is part of the environment to mould and to be moulded by the dwellers. This moulding is part of the activity of dwelling.

Dwelling can be seen as the creation of personal environments. In this sense we are diametrically opposed to the modernism of Le Corbusier. Indeed the concern with dwelling is to locate this discourse within the milieu of the postmodern. According to Lyotard (1984) the postmodern can be seen as a move away from an intrinsic characterisation of things towards an understanding of what the thing does in the lives of those who own or use it. It is where we stop asking ourselves "is it true?" and instead ask "what use is it?" This functionality, however, cannot be abstracted into a universal question, but can rather only be determined personally. Thus a postmodern description would be to stress difference and anti-essentialism. As Lyotard has stated, postmodern is an "incredulity towards metanarratives" (1984, p. xxiv). It is where the totalising visions of modernity are seen as absolutely implausible. There is no universal or necessary condition, merely options that individuals can take according to their constraints, perceptions, expectations, etc. Moreover knowledge is now diffused and diffusing — "Postmodern knowledge is not simply a tool of the authorities; it refines our sensitivity to differences and reinforces our ability to tolerate the incommensurable" (Lyotard, 1984, p. xx). Postmodern knowledge is something that cannot be controlled centrally, but is rather diffused amongst individuals within the community. It thus expresses itself in diverse and differentiated ways.

At the centre of the postmodern is the recognition of alterity — of the needs and perceptions of others who are different and perhaps irreconcilable to us. It is to recognise that others may not be categorised according to our criteria; that to universalise is to impose our view on the unwilling other. Thus a postmodern conception is to be aware that, in as much as we have personal needs and perceptions which give our life meaning, then so do others. We thus have a responsibility to the other. This responsibility is absolute (Levinas, 1969), even when we are faced by those who are foreign to us (Derrida, 1993). It is through the significance of our personal environment that we recognise its significance to the other.

Goodchild (1991) has related this postmodern concern for the personal with housing design. He stated that a house only acquires meaning as a home when it is personalised. This implies that the individual should have some control over the dwelling. Moreover the design of any dwelling should "consider the personal characteristics and lifestyles of likely users" (p. 134). The meaning attached through personalisation "suggests the existence of significant social differences in environmental perception"(p. 134). Goodchild goes further to suggest that the home is "an expression of personal identity" (p. 135) and therefore perception can be said to go beyond the associative to the personal. The perception of the dwelling as a personal embodiment is crucial, even if the individuality is expressed according to social norms of popular taste.

However, a concentration of housing as a noun neglects the personal within the process of dwelling for the supposedly wider concerns of policy. Housing becomes the tool of policy, rather than policy being the tool of our need to dwell. This is because of the linkage of housing to economic policy, where the latter is allowed to dominate. This situation derives out of a totalising view of human nature that perceives humans as being rational, self-interested, and thus motivated towards the accumulation of property. It is the attempt to create the property owning democracy. One of the aims of this essay is to suggest that this perception of human nature is an over-simplification. Individuals do not necessarily operate in predictable and pre-patterned ways. Markets are used to mitigate their own potentially adverse affects. Individuals play in the market (and may do so positively) so as to insulate themselves and their families from its impersonality and its implacability.

The supposed virtues of a market system are the very things that households use the mechanisms of the market to avoid.

If such a totalising view is unsatisfactory, it is then advisable to withdraw from the very attempt to describe and determine human behaviour. However, is it possible to place a concept in its stead that is not itself totalising and categorical with regard to behaviour? How are we to avoid merely replacing one totalising project with another? I shall suggest that this aim might be achieved by the setting of limits. The roles of government, housing professionals, and other outside interests should be strictly prescribed to ensure that the dwellers themselves are empowered to control their own dwelling environment. This suggests that a thorough rethink is necessary regarding what it is possible for housing policy to realistically achieve.

It also suggests that a rethink about the nature of housing studies and housing research is also necessary. Housing research has been characterised by a narrow empiricism (Kemeny, 1992b) concerned with the issues of aggregate production and consumption. Housing research sees its role as observing current systems of provision and consumption, criticising them and offering proposals for reform based on these observation. By and large (with the recent exceptions of writers such as Gurney, 1990; 1991, Kemeny, 1992a; 1992b and Somerville, 1994) this situation is seen as largely unproblematic. As Kemeny (1992b) has observed it is not an area of discourse much taken up with self reflection.

Academic housing discourse can be seen as sharing the same concerns as housing policy. Indeed the two feed off each other, with policy initiatives offering the possibility for observation and critique, and research offering legitimacy to policy. Therefore housing discourse can be implicated in the charge of policy failure. It therefore needs to become aware of the necessary limitations that should bound it, in terms of what researchers may legitimately say and what is their responsibility for the aporias at the heart of policy. In short housing research must become a more reflexive field of enquiry that becomes more aware of its conceptual and analytical tools and the problematic that surrounds them. This can only be done by appreciating the proper

limitations that are and, equally important, should be placed around
housing discourse.

The purpose of this essay is to attempt to state where the limits in
policy and discourse are. It will offer a detailed critique of contemporary housing policy — what I shall call *modern* — and place an
alternative description in its stead based on an anti-essentialist and anti-
realist epistemic. It offers little in the way of empirical data or evidence,
but is rather a critique of current housing policy and the ways in which
it is observed and described. It attempts to offer a tentative outline of
both an alternative policy framework, and a programme for future
housing research. It therefore suggests what policy and discourse
should be about. Therefore the book aims to set an agenda rather than
to "prove" anything.

As the subtitle of the book suggests this is a philosophical investigation. It may strike some as odd that housing is seen as a pertinent
subject for philosophical discourse. Indeed, as stated above, it is an area
that has been largely immune from the reflexive practice necessary for
philosophical discussion. It is more common to suggest that the purpose of housing policy and housing discourse is to get more houses, or
more likely, "homes", built. Accordingly an overly abstract or philosophical treatment of housing is derided as being either pretentious or irrelevant.
What is seen as more important is production and consumption — the
number of housing starts, tenure distribution and polarities, the cost of
development and the subsidisation of consumption, etc. Of course these
issues are important, but there are only of limited usefulness without an
understanding of the principles — or limits — that determine them. No
one would seriously suggest that the sole concern of the medical profes-
sion should be the numbers treated, nor that the sole concern of
educationalists should be for the numbers educated. Medical professionals
and academics, including moral philosophers, are rightly concerned about
the ethics of issues such as abortion, gene therapy and the quality of life.
Likewise educationalists, including philosophers of education, are concerned with issues about what is taught to children and why, and indeed
how children are capable of learning anything at all. These are issues
and concerns that can be dated to both the birth of medicine and educa-

tion as distinct practices, and as philosophy as a distinct means of enquiry about the physical and social worlds.

There are possible reasons for this distinction between medicine,
education and housing. Perhaps the most persuasive one is that housing
— or for much of human history, shelter — has only recently become
distinguished from the elemental practices of our daily lives. As both
Heidegger (1993) and Illich (1992) have suggested dwelling means to
live as humans in the world. It is the art of surviving in an environment.
Thus for much of human history it has not been distinct from our
everyday practices. Unlike education and, most certainly, medicine it
has only recently become separated from our everyday practices. It is
perhaps this proximity to the primordial nature of shelter that ensures
we still see housing as merely a physical entity. It is the very *taken-for-
grantedness* of housing as physical space that hides its existentiality.

Of course, it should not be forgotten that there has long been a
philosophy of architecture as a branch of aesthetics, but this has, until
recently, been concerned with the aesthetics of architecture as public
space or as luxury consumption. The very transcendent nature of the
aesthetics of architecture has divorced it from the ubiquity of the personal dwelling. The philosophy of architecture is thus no more related
to housing than the philosophy of painting.

A further reason for the neglect of a philosophical approach for
housing is the very narrow concerns that have dominated policy and
the field of housing studies. Post war policy has largely been concerned
with the provision of public or so called "social" housing. Much of
housing research has quite understandably followed this policy approach. Therefore the concentration has been on providing for a
specific group perceived as having pressing needs. Indeed the term
"housing need" is almost always related to those deemed to be inade-
quately housed. This differs markedly from the near universality of
health and educational provision. The latter public services are open to
all, whilst housing is seen as being for certain groups only. Moreover
this means that there is a separation between the users on the one hand
and policy makers and researchers on the other. Medical and educational researchers will generally have or can expect to use the provision

— they operate within it as consumers. Housing researchers generally do not receive the outputs of housing policy — they are not the consumers of policy (or at least not the areas of policy they are professionally concerned with). This places a limitation on the potential reflexivity on the part of the researcher.

Thus for whatever reason, there has been a lack of philosophical discourse on housing. The result has been a neglect, for instance, of the existential quality of housing and the political and ideological impact that policy has on the perception of dwellers. It is the contention of this essay that this neglect is one of the major reasons for the failure of housing policy. The concentration is with the short term view that sees today's policy as solving the failures of the immediate past; that meeting housing need is a technical issue determined by building better and more. This, I shall show merely replicates the problems of yesterday. Therefore we should begin to think why, and for whom we are building; and whether those we decide it is for actually need what we assume they do.

This essay aims to focus on these issues. It seeks to widen the focus of housing research beyond the provision for a particular group in need to look at the significance that housing has more generally. This is not an attempt to downplay the housing need of the disadvantaged, but rather to suggest that they can be best helped by broadening the appreciation of needs and capabilities and thus allowing them and others to fulfil these *on their terms* free from the intervention of the centralising tendencies in policy and discourse.

Thus a philosophical approach need not be either pretentious or irrelevant, but rather one that offers to broaden and deepen discourse on housing.

PART ONE

THE PROBLEM

WITH HOUSING

CHAPTER ONE

THE SIGNIFICANCE OF HOUSING

1.1. Standards, Aggregates and Perception

Housing policy has consistently been concerned with a material aggregation of dwellings. When housing policy is unravelled it is seen to emphasise material standards and the technical issues of control and management of the stock of dwellings. It is basically a concern for the number of dwellings of a particular type. Thus housing need is about placing households in suitable dwellings according to some ranking criteria. Housing management is about the maintenance of the stock of dwellings and the harmonisation of this stock with the perceived needs of those aspiring to live in it.

A household is defined as homeless not necessarily because of an absolute lack of housing but because their current housing has failed to match a particular standard. Indeed a family sharing with another household, who would otherwise be under-occupying the property, may be defined as statutorily homeless despite the amenities available in the dwelling. We need not be lacking housing to be statutorily homeless (nor, of course, are we statutorily homeless merely because we lack a dwelling).

A household is determined as living in overcrowded conditions by statute, despite their own feelings towards their current housing. They may find this dwelling suits their needs because of its proximity to family, employment and community. However, the only relevant consideration is the formal standard that constitutes overcrowding.

Standards of behaviour are also circumscribed. Public sector landlords, consistent with current law and practice, insist on certain behaviour from tenants which go somewhat further than the obligation to pay rent by the due date and not to damage the property. Behaviour, such as relations with neighbours is controlled by tenancy clauses on nuisance and noise. In this manner the landlord seeks to control the private behaviour of households in their own home.

These three concepts — homelessness, overcrowding and nuisance — share a similar quality. They are all concerned with personal rather than public effects. Despite the fact that homelessness is a national issue, its primary effects are on those who directly suffer from it. The same can be said for overcrowding and nuisance. They can all be seen as part of a general attempt to prescribe standards for situations and behaviour that are personal and, because we would not expect uniformity from distinct individuals, are likely to be infinitely variable.

Housing policy is concerned with aggregates. Policy looks at the housing needs of the country, identifies national problems and goes on to posit national solutions. The emphasis of policy, be it the Attlee government, the Conservative governments of the 1950s, or the Thatcher/Major administrations, the main concern is with the numbers of houses built and the amount of money spent in achieving these targets (Daunton, 1987; Malpass and Murie, 1994). It is seen as an acceptable reply to questions on the plight of the homeless to state that the government is spending more money "in real terms" this year than last.

The number of housing starts is seen as a key economic indicator. The rise or fall in house prices — aggregated regardless of area or type — are seen as significant both of economic activity and as a determinant of consumer confidence. It is stated that the economy cannot recover from recession until the housing market recovers and house prices rise again. Yet others believe that consumers will not re-enter the housing market until their confidence is buoyed up by economic recovery. What is agreed however is that house prices — as opposed to the price of *my house* — are significant on the behaviour of consumers. It is significant as an aggregated national asset.

Housing is perceived largely in economic terms, as an indicator of the level of activity in the national economy. Housing policy is thus essentially part of economic policy. It is a means of attaining national policy targets whether those be the creation of full employment, the stimulation of demand through government spending or individual empowerment and the furthering of popular capitalism.

The post-1979 Conservative governments have particularly emphasised the economic nature of housing. They have done this through maintaining the significance of housing as a macro-economic indicator, but also through a heightening of the micro-economic effects of home ownership. National housing policy under the Thatcher and Major administrations has increased private consumption through measures such as the Right-to-Buy and a policy of running down the public sector. This is micro-economic policy, in that it is an attempt to moderate individual behaviour, yet with avowedly macro-economic, and indeed macro-political effects. It has served to enhance the privatisation of the economy and to heighten the influence of market based distribution. Thus housing has been commodified through its relation to a market as the primary means of allocation.

Housing according to this thesis can be seen as significant for three reasons. Firstly, because it allows households access to a particular standard of living seen as essential as a minimum standard (the fact that it may be an aspiration rather than a realisation is not especially relevant to policy formulation). Secondly, housing is significant as a macro-economic indicator, and, thirdly, as an economic good which allows households access to markets. The political significance of housing is thus derived essentially from the material and the economic.

However, is this really all the significance housing has? Is it merely reducible to material and economic well being? We can give an immediate answer by suggesting that the significance of housing is that it is *a means to an end, rather than being an end in itself*. It is a means of fulfilment that allows other human activities to take place (Birchall, 1988; Turner, 1972, 1976).

There are a myriad of ends to which housing may assist as the means of fulfilment. For the architect it can fulfil certain aesthetic functions towards the creation of a work of art. For the household it could be seen as a means of shelter, privacy and security allowing them to pursue their intimate relationships and order their private lives as they wish. Alternatively it could be a means to a capital gain, where housing is an appreciating asset and thus a creator of wealth, either for the particular owner or their children. For planners it could be a means of social engineering aimed perhaps at achieving a differentiated urban order through zoning of urban functions, or alternatively through the interaction of diverse communities. For politicians housing is a means to achieve particular political ends. In the case of the Thatcher and Major administrations it furthers an ideology of choice, independence and moral responsibility through markets. Previous governments have seen housing as a means of equalising distribution through the provision of high quality subsidised dwellings. Thus, whilst there may be no consensus on ends, it is general for housing to act as a means towards fulfilling an end or ends. Therefore the perception of housing as being economically significant is merely one possibility.

The fact it is a perception adds a further dimension to this discussion on means and ends. By perceiving housing as an economic good, with an apparently intrinsic value as a tradable asset, it becomes an end in itself. Housing, for the household — but not for the politicians pursuing the policy — takes on an intrinsic quality. It becomes synonymous with its value, and thus when its value declines, the end — or usefulness — of the house declines. This is where housing is seen as significant because of the property rights one enjoys over it. It is where ownership takes precedence over use, and thus it becomes an end in itself.

There is here an interesting dichotomy regarding the national and personal significance of housing. Individuals own this property, not the state. Indeed policy is an attempt to transfer ownership from public to private. There is thus a national policy aiming to have a national effect, which operates by affecting the individual's perception of the significance of housing. Thus there is a duality whereby housing is resignified for the individual as an end in itself, in order to achieve the political ends of a national government. Individual ends become the means that government uses to fulfil a particular policy.

The issue of perception is indeed an important one. It is often not the significance of housing per se that is important, but rather the perception of its significance. Housing is being used as a means to achieve the "property owning democracy", yet in doing so it becomes perceived as significant in itself. Thus the role of ideology is emerging as central to any understanding of the significance of housing. Housing policy hinges upon how ideology determines the perceptions of all the players in the policy framework. It is indeed the effect of ideology that creates the paradox of housing as having an intrinsic significance. Ideology thus is central to descriptions of housing policy.

1.2. The Method of Housing Studies

Housing studies as a discipline of research, description and analysis has tended to concentrate on the material and on aggregates. It has largely concerned itself with issues of production and consumption. In short, it could be characterised as the study of housing markets or systems. Housing is perceived as being an aggregate with particular standards of amenity necessary to fulfil particular needs. Of course these aggregations of need are themselves determined by the aggregate standards of the national stock. Thus housing discourse creates its own self fulfilling problematic.

Housing discourse, including academic housing studies, has naturally mirrored the formulation of policy. Gurney (1991) contends that this mirroring is because of the epistemic base of housing studies. As a discipline it "has traditionally drawn on political science, social administration and sociolgy for its cues"(1991, p. 4). It has thus been flavoured by the predominant structuralist epistemologies of these disciplines with their concerns for the structural determinants of social action and with the constraints and possibilities determined by a social structure.

However, Gurney places his discussion on the epistemics of housing studies around research into the meaning of the home that has been a focus in housing studies from the late 1980s onwards (Gurney, 1990; Saunders, 1990; Saunders and Williams, 1988; Somerville, 1989, 1993). He sees an "epistemic drift" away from "the metanarratives of Althusserian structuralism" into "micro-analysis" (1991, p.4). The concern for aggregates is beginning to fragment into a discussion on the meaning of housing to the individual. Hence the increasing focus on the home as an area of research.

However, Gurney is uncertain as to whether housing studies,

dependent on its traditional disciplines, is capable of offering many insights because of the methodological constraints it has imposed upon itself. He is unsure whether such a micro-analysis is not best left to psychology and phenomenology.

Thus Gurney offers what appears to be an important dichotomy — between metanarratives and micro-analysis — but seems to deny that housing studies can take advantage of it because of its structuralist bias. Whilst he is certainly correct in seeing the limitations of much of housing research, I would suggest that he is too pessimistic in his assessment of the potential for housing studies to be "re-invented" to take advantage of other disciplines, including those of psychology and phenomenology. Indeed Gurney's own work (1990) is evidence of the fruitful links housing studies can make with psychology, phenomenology and social theory. Therefore we should not dismiss the ability of housing studies to develop into new avenues, but rather seek to demonstrate the insights that may be gained from them.

Indeed the development of a micro-analytical approach to housing studies appears essential in assessing the dichotomy between the national and individual significance of housing. I believe we should therefore look beyond the traditional disciplines where necessary, but without rejecting them when they are useful. What is necessary, however, is to beware of mainstream structuralist metanarratives.

Such descriptions concentrate on aggregates. Political studies of housing have tended to concentrate on the political structures as a whole (Malpass & Means, 1993; Malpass et al, 1993). Where particular institutions are considered they are done so in relation to the state. They have not tended to consider the role and practice of individuals within the system. Micro-economic studies of housing, whilst purporting to consider individual behaviour do so only in its generality (e.g., Albon & Stafford, 1987). They consider the rational consumer as an ideal type and not as a psychologically complex being. There is no attempt to examine the role of the individuals as differentiated and incommensurable in their aims and actions.

A further problem with much of housing research is its attribution of agency to institutions such as government and the state and to all encompassing narratives such as capitalism. It is as if capitalism is capable of deliberative acts on behalf of particular groups, or against the interests of others. However, throughout such analyses there is no appreciation given as to how capitalism co-ordinates this activity. It is as if there are rational explicit relations acting with the predictability of laws, that relate "social forces" to institutions, groups and individuals. It is thus not the actions of a particular government minister or official that affects a particular situation, but rather there is a seemingly all encompassing "plan" in which any one action is seemingly an inevitable part (a particular example of this is the marxist analysis of working class housing by Damer, 1989).

Moral agency is given to the institution of government itself, as if decisions are not taken by individuals within the institution. Government is seen to act as a whole, because of measurable pressures and forces, rather than action being as a result of individual judgement, mistakes or prejudice. The government is thus seen as greater than the sum of its parts and, furthermore, is given a moral existence of its own. Such a position serves to deny individual responsibility for actions and their consequences within government. Moreover it tends to categorise individual action within the rubric of institutional agency. Thus individuals can be characterised by type according to the institution or structural interests they are identified with. Individuals are not responsible except as examples of their class or as representatives of particular metanarratives.

Weil (1987) has discussed this relationship between individuals and structural interests. She refuses to grant moral agency to the group: "(o)bligations are only binding on human beings. There are no obligations on collectivities as such" (1987, p. 4). Collectivities and institutions have no moral agency. Instead it is vested with those individuals within the collectivity. These obligations however fall on both the private part and that part of the individual that relates to leadership, co-operation and service within the collective. Obligations, and thus the granting of moral purpose, are placed on the part of the sum, and the latter thus has no meaning when stripped of individual obligation. The group is therefore merely the sum of its morally active parts. It is an agglomeration of these parts and has no identity separate of it. Deliberative acts come from individuals and not from institutions and metanarratives.

This is not, however, to suggest a form of atomism whereby there can be no interrelationship between individuals. It is rather to say that relations are made up of expectations and perceptions. Group activity is thus the sum of individual action and relationships based on their interacting expectations and perceptions.

The reason for the attribution of agency to structures and metanarratives is because of the desire to contain phenomena within the bounds of metadiscourse (Lyotard, 1984). An attempt is made to control the meaning of political and social action by abstracting it into a format of predictive behaviour. In so doing generalisations can be made that allow political action to be "understood". Thus models and ideal types are constructed as to how the political system operates that seek to eradicate contingency and the unexpected and therefore allow these generalisations to be perpetuated. Items that do not fit into the model are dismissed as irrelevant and ignored. Thus the model becomes both rigid and self-perpetuating as the arbiter not just of the significance of events and practices, but of reality itself. Economic reality is determined by models of the economic world that impose predictive "laws" onto behaviour. These "laws" become self-perpetuating because they themselves filter the perception of behaviour. Moreover behaviour that occurs outside of the model is ignored as insignificant because the model does not accept it.

The structuralist epistemic is widespread amongst the social sciences. As an example Shackle (1992) has shown how economics, through adopting a form of positivist scientific rationalism, has actually misunderstood the complexity of individual economic behaviour:

> The field of economic events has been assumed to be self-contained and self-sufficient, shut off from the rest of humanity's affairs by a wall of rationality. Economic science has been assumed to resemble the basic sciences of Nature, where ultimately everything that might be reduced to, or explained by, a single and solitary 'secret of the cosmos'. (1992, p.4)

Economics is seen to be a complete autonomous discipline offering a total answer. It is what Lyotard (1984) referred to as a *metadiscourse*. The total answer can be attempted through the assumption of rationality. Shackle, however, questions how rationality is obtained in practice. Is it sufficient to merely assume perfect knowledge or ought economists to consider how humans obtain it? Without perfect knowledge rational decisions are not possible and thus the whole edifice begins to crumble.

Shackle believes that economic behaviour should be about human thoughts and deeds, not a concern for what he terms "the ultimate chemistry of man" (1992, p.4). It is as much a concern for how perceptions and expectations affect behaviour as the behaviour itself. However, this concern is infinitely complex and unpredictable. It is therefore not containable and this is the reason why rationalist assumptions persist. They allow economists to maintain the fiction of predicting behaviour, but only at the expense of misunderstanding the dynamics of social action.

This pre-occupation for rationality is seen throughout the social sciences and within housing studies. A particular recent example of this is found in the work of Kemeny (1992b). This work attempts to integrate housing studies into the wider social science corpus. In doing so he provides one of the few attempts to analyse the nature, state and prospects of academic housing discourse. In this sense Kemeny's work is of particular significance.

Kemeny argues that:

> A central problem of much of housing studies is that it retains a myopic and narrow focus on housing policy and housing markets and neglects broader issues. Housing studies is still too isolated from debates and theories in the other social sciences and what is needed now is further integration into these. (p. xv)

Furthermore, he suggests that housing studies exists "out of the context of society as a whole" (p. ix), to the effect that "Housing is one of those subject-determined fields that all too easily becomes an unreflexive empirical study in abstraction from society as a whole" (p. xvi). Housing studies thus is seen as having a narrow focus that is separated from the social world and the purpose of Kemeny's book is "to further the theoretical development of housing research" (p. xvi). Thus far Kemeny appears to be agreeing with the general tenor of my critique of housing discourse. He sees that much of housing research is unreflexive, yet, because of his embeddedness in current housing discourse, he cannot break out beyond the narrow confines of the field itself. Kemeny appears able to see the need for greater reflexivity, yet is himself guilty of the insularity he criticises. This insularity can be shown by a reading of some of Kemeny's statements.

Firstly, to deal with Kemeny's argument on its own terms, he suggests that housing has been abstracted out of the social structure by the narrow empiricism of housing studies and his aim is to re-integrate housing. According to Kemeny housing studies is not a theoretical field as it cannot seek to determine the relations between housing and the social structure. As such it is separated off from the mainstream social science disciplines. However, as Kemeny himself states, "disciplines are based on a process of conceptual abstraction" (p. 4). We must presume that these concepts are attempts to model the social structure and social reality. Theories, if they are to be of any substantive use, are abstractions from the social world aimed at assisting in the understanding of that world. Therefore, in modelling the social, the social sciences necessarily abstract out of the social themselves. In this sense Kemeny appears to be suggesting that housing discourse is abstracting out of an abstraction of the social. This may mean it is not a theoretical field, but does not necessarily imply anything with regard to housing studies. Thus housing, according to Kemeny, can only be understood within an abstract model of the social world.

But we can question Kemeny's discourse on more fundamental grounds, namely his apparent failure to recognise that housing discourse is itself a socially created process. It neither is, nor can be, separated from the social world it seeks to describe and analyse. A discipline or field cannot be abstracted from the social, for where else is it created and maintained? The process of housing discourse, including institutions, academics, texts, etc, exists within current power structures which serve to determine, maintain and constrain this discourse. Indeed Kemeny hints at this when he states that housing studies is becoming institutionalised within the academic environment. The difficulty appears to be the way in which Kemeny conceptualises the notion of social structure itself. He appears to be referring to a particular model entitled "the social structure". Thus, in common with the structuralist epistemic I have already cited, Kemeny has reified a particular model — in this case of the social structure — and thus feels able to separate academic enquiry from the context in which it exists. This is not to suggest that Kemeny adheres to the "Althusserian structuralism" characterised by Gurney (1991) — although, as I shall show below, he does tend to favour structure over agency — but rather that he maintains the rule bound abstraction identified by Shackle (1992) as bedevilling social theory. Kemeny's structuralism is thus methodological rather than an adherence to a deterministic social theory.

Any discussion on the reflexivity of a field or discipline needs to understand the limitations of such practice. Discourse, as Derrida (1978) has suggested, cannot escape its epistemological boundaries. In as much as discourses on irrationality are bound by the rationality of discourse, and therefore are understandable, so a discourse based on conceptual abstraction must also be tied to particular social determinants. Without these determinants there can be nothing to abstract from. Epistemology is definitionally social, for how else does it contain meaning? Thus the epistemological framework of any discourse ensures it is referenced to the social world.

The particular limitation of Kemeny's argument is that it appears to lead to the conclusion that a more theoretically developed housing discourse is an end in itself. He seem to see that housing theory and research are justified as existents worthy of merit in themselves. This would have two consequences. Firstly, as I have already shown, it implies a deliberative structuring towards the abstraction from society as a whole. It would be merely to ingrain a hermetic context in which reflexivity is determined by the epistemic of housing studies. Secondly, through the concepts of discrete concepts and forms of analysis, it would lead to the very institutionalisation, and thus epistemic separation, that Kemeny is trying to avoid by making housing discourse more theoretically sophisticated.

This situation is compounded by Kemeny's attempt to define housing studies. In doing so he shows how housing discourse mirrors the concern with the material and with aggregates. According to Kemeny, housing studies is concerned with physical and technical issues:

> Housing studies is clearly about housing. But this tells us little. Housing, after all, in its simplest and crudest sense, is the bricks and mortar or other building material that comprise the constructions within which people live. But as a field within the social sciences, housing research equally clearly involves the examination of the social, economic, political and other relationships that centre on housing. We might, therefore, by way of providing a starting point, provisionally define housing studies as *the study of the social, political, economic, cultural and other institutions and relationships that constitute the provision and utilisation of dwellings.* (p. 8, my emphasis)

The first point to note is that Kemeny defines housing studies in terms of structure and, consequently, downplays the role of individual agency. For Kemeny it is the study of particular institutions and relationships that lead to the provision and utilisation of dwellings. There is no reference to the role of households, nor to the significance of the home. Instead it sees structures as the determining factor.

Whilst the role of structures cannot be ignored, we need to integrate the role of the household and individual agents into housing discourse. Dwellings, which are provided through processes of social interaction, are boundaries for individual lives. The majority of housing is not occupied socially, but privately. Therefore the relation between the dwelling and the dweller, which is not reducible to a structural analysis, must be considered within housing discourse.

Kemeny's definition, by defining relationships in abstract terms, locates the significance of housing at the macro level. The implication of the terminology, with its references to the social, political, economic and cultural, is of a discourse at the level of the assumed homogeneous communities bounded by the state. This becomes particularly apparent with his prioritisation of production above consumption.

One can also question whether Kemeny's definition takes the discussion much further than the simple and crude sense of housing as bricks and mortar. What is provision concerned with if not "the bricks and mortar or other building materials that comprise the constructions within which people live" (p. 8)? What else is Kemeny suggesting is being provided other than constructions? By placing the emphasis on provision he conflates the social, political, economic and cultural significance of housing to that of providing physical constructions. This is to reduce housing discourse to the level of the economics of housebuilding.

The categories to which Kemeny apportions significance are also problematical. Ignoring the catch-all phrase "and other", he identifies the significant factors as the social, political, economic and cultural institutions and relationships. However, because he is only concerned with the macro level, he has ignored several layers of significance that contribute to the provision and utilisation of dwellings. There are several missing factors that need to be discussed such as the role of perception, the emotions and the personal psychological effects of phenomena. We are not able to understand the notions of belonging, identification and physical and ontological security through Kemeny's general categories. Whilst they can be said to fall generally within the category of the cultural, this does not help us to deal with the phenomena located at the personal level within the household within the dwelling.

Kemeny clearly sees no problem in distinguishing between the notion of provision and utilisation. However, these terms are not exclusive to each other, but rather utilisation is in part determined by the form of provision and type of provision. Utilisation can be enhanced or circumscribed by such issues as security of tenure or permanence, standard of amenity and access. Thus the nature of what is provided conditions the utilisation. Furthermore it is necessary to differentiate between the use of the term "utilisation" as a social resource in the sense of the efficient use and management of national resources, and as a term relating to the manner in which a household is able to use its own dwelling. Only the former usage — as a macro level concept

— is amenable to Kemeny's concern for the social, political, economic and cultural.

Kemeny's focus is thus a narrow one that restricts housing studies to a macro level discourse of provision and utilisation. It is a focus on the material and how it comes to bear on households. It implies that housing affects individual households and credits them with no part in the determination of their dwelling environment. This is particularly apparent in his rejection of the consumption approach to housing discourse put forward by Saunders and Williams (1988).

Saunders and Williams see the home as a neglected area of research within the literature on the sociology and political economy of housing. In particular they attempt to link the home to the sociology of consumption that they can see developing. They contend that there is an increasing recognition that production does not play such a "central role as sociological and marxist analyses have generally imagined" (p. 81). The home is portrayed as a particular focus of consumption for households.

Kemeny sees that the problem of such a consumption approach is that it avoids rather than resolves the "conceptual ambiguities surrounding the relationship between dwelling and household" (p. 9). Kemeny's point is that these concepts, which are central to any discussion of the home, are often defined in terms of each other. The term "household" is used to define the term "dwelling", and vice versa. Whilst I would agree with Kemeny that Saunders and Williams do appear to skirt this problem, it is somewhat perverse to criticise them when discourse based on provision commits the same error not only with regard to the notions of household and dwelling, but also with regard to the connection between provision and utilisation. In this sense the provision thesis is at least as guilty of a lack of conceptual clarity, if not more so. Thus Kemeny's comment is not so much a valid criticism as a diversion.

Kemeny's criticism of the consumption approach is particularly deficient in that he actually offers no substantive grounds for his criticism. He suggests simply that it would lead to a narrowing of the research focus of housing studies as it would ignore the macro level and the effect of the embeddedness of housing in the social structure. He appears to suggest that the home exists outside of the social structure. Kemeny's model of the social structure seems to consist of a unitary public sphere in which the private realm is excluded. Whilst he is correct to warn against an overemphasis on the micro level, the effect is the apparent preferencing of the macro to the exclusion of the micro level. He does not apparently perceive the social structure (or rather social structures) as consisting of layers of relations, institutions and structures around individuals and collectivities that are interdependent, co-determining and co-substantive. As I have previously stated there can be no area that is outside or beyond the social — it is definitionally inclusive. This does not imply that the personal and the private do not exist, rather that they exist within, and as an integral part of, the social.

Essentially I want to suggest that Kemeny sees the debate between his position and that of researchers such as Saunders and Williams as being a dichotomy that needs to be decided in favour of one and to the exclusion of the other. He is suggesting that housing discourse may only have one substantive focus, and, of course, he favours his own view to the exclusion of micro level discourses. My concern then is not whether Saunders and Williams offer a "better" description of the housing process, and certainly not whether it is the "true" one, but rather to suggest that Kemeny's attempt to put housing studies on the "right path" is misguided.

What I seek to emphasise in answer to Kemeny is that there are no substantive grounds to suggest that there should be only one focus for housing discourse. Indeed a wide and diverse focus for housing studies would strengthen rather than weaken housing discourse. There is every reason to believe that a singularity of purpose within a field of study would encourage the very insularity that Kemeny is so concerned to eradicate. Kemeny appears to want a more theoretically aware housing studies, but only if it becomes more aware of a rule bound and abstract sociology of production.

Somerville (1994), in his recent attempt to develop a typology of housing discourse, has shown that there is a diversity of approaches within housing studies. Somerville suggests four distinct types of explanations of housing policy; systems of actors, hypothetico-deductive, realist and culturalist (which includes Kemeny's discourse). The types of explanation are differentiated in terms of distinct ontology, epistemology and methodology.

However, whilst such an approach is useful in showing the similarities and, for my purposes, the distinctions between various explanations, there is a danger that this typology can be used as a control mechanism. Certain explanations can only be used to support others if they fall within the same type. Moreover once an explanation is located within a particular type it may be summarily dismissed as having the same failings as others within that type. In this sense the drawing up of typologies may potentially arrest the development of open and questioning discourses on housing policy. Thus the effect of Somerville's typology is to further codify the rule bound nature of academic housing studies.

Therefore instead of using a typology as a means of controlling discourse, we should see the diversity described by Somerville as a source of possibility. We should seek to develop links between these various types of discourse instead of seeing them as distinct and separated paths.

I have concentrated primarily on Kemeny not because I see his work as being particularly deficient, but rather because it is a significant attempt to develop academic housing discourse. He has set off a debate about the nature of housing studies that is now being responded to. Yet his work is still within the narrow confines of an epistemic that sees housing in terms of the material and aggregates. Thus, in showing the limitations in a work at the vanguard of theoretical debate about housing discourse, I have tried to show the deficiencies in housing discourse itself. I have shown how it attempts to focus research towards macro level notion that concentrates on provision and utilisation which merely serves to reinforce the perception of housing policy as being concerned with material aggregations.

This macro level discourse rests on an epistemology dependent on the notion of progress towards a universally applicable solution. The assumption is that there is a particular foundation upon which discourse rests. It is this foundationalism (Rorty, 1980) or *metaphysical essentialism* that has overridden any attempt within housing studies to describe the practice of living as individuated and contingent. To depart from this foundationalist path is to risk being accused of using an unscientific methodology. However, the point that ought to be constantly presented is how to establish procedures, scientific or otherwise, that allow us to deal with what are plural and often incommensurable practices.

There are thus limitations with housing research and discourse and we therefore should look towards other methods such as phenomenology when they are useful. This will allow an appreciation of the role of the individual to develop through concentrating on issues of consciousness, perception and expectations. Housing researchers need to be better able to describe individual moral agency and its relation to group, community and institution, and they should be prepared to use methods that allow them to do this. Housing studies, therefore needs not only to be more reflexive, but also more open ended. However, they should not neglect the opportunity of integrating the mainstream analyses of politics, sociology and economics when they can assist in the development a rounded discourse about the processes of dwelling within the environment.

This appreciation of individual perception and expectations opens up the potential for developing an analytic of politics that encapsulates individual agency. This can be seen as a micro-politics that centres on individual, rather than social action, or, more precisely, how an individual negotiates into or out of particular social action and what roles are possible within the vernacular environment and the particular institutions that operate within it. It is a concern for the local as opposed to the national, and for the small instead of the grand. If politics is seen as power exercised within and through relationships (where moral agency is equated with legitimate power), we can posit a concept of power at the micro level. This is where power is exercised individually, or within the direct environment of the individual, through the ability of the individual to mediate and moderate their local environment. This, of course, will involve both individual and co-operative action.

Such an analysis is not an attempt to build a model of predication, but is rather one of description, not only of practice, but of possibility. Therefore what I seek to identify are the limits of conceptualisation and the centrality of contingency in this practice and possibility. In order to do so I shall develop a mode of discourse that is anti-essentialist. I have already made use of the distinction between modernism and postmodernism as a basic framework in order to differentiate between a universalising discourse, as put forward by Le Corbusier, and a more fragmentary and diverse discourse that allows for personalisation within the dwelling process. Whilst this is a useful distinction, and the theses presented in this essay should be seen within the general milieu of the postmodern, it is perhaps insufficient to rely on this broad dichotomy to justify a method of analysis. The postmodern is apparently definitionally opaque to definition, largely because it is most often presented in opposition to what it is not. It is that which is *after* or *beyond* the modern. Thus it aims to counter universalism, totalist discourses and metaphysical presence. Yet its very characterisation as a reaction to the aporias of modernity means that any critique of modernity, that does not simply hark back to the premodern, tends to be labelled postmodern. This means that the term postmodern can be used as a catch all to include what are infact disconnected critiques and discourses. Whilst there is nothing worng, and indeed everything to gain, in bringing disparate discourses together, to put them all under the heading of postmodern militates both against the distinctiveness of the particular coupling and the notion of postmodernity as a meaningful term of reference. Indeed Rorty, who has been one of the philosophers most closely identified with postmodernism, has ceased to describe himself as a postmodernist because of the apparent lack of coherence of the concept (Rorty, 1991b). Rorty found it impossible to link so-called postmodernists in literature with those in architecture or in philosophy. He has thus become "hesitant about attempts to periodise culture" (1991b, p. 1), preferring instead to periodise within disciplines and genres. Likewise Kolb (1992) also warns against seeing culture as a linear progression from the premodern to the modern and on to the postmodern. This apparent process is just one more example of modernity's universalism that seeks to categorise and quantify all phenomena.

Thus to define this discourse as merely postmodern would be beg many questions about the exact nature of my endeavour. Instead I seek an approach that is consistent with the diversity and incommensurability of postmodernism in its generality, but which will give a more precise format in which to place both the following critique of current housing policy and the alternative I shall seek to present.

1.3. A Libertarian Methodology

If we are accept the criticism of universalising descriptions then there are certain steps we may not take. These centre, firstly, on the notions of proof and refutation — whether we can force our arguments onto another and destroy their position — and, secondly, on the issue of outcomes. Can we theorise to propose a particular end, or must we be limited to description or redescription? These two related issues have been discussed by Nozick (1974; 1981). I shall, in discussing Nozick, be wary of some of his conclusions and rather concentrate on the methodological tools he has developed to reach them. However, I shall not be able to avoid his substantive ideas in their entirety. This, of course, is because there is a fairly direct link between the methodology and the outcomes of Nozick's deliberations. However, this linkage does not preclude me from taking elements of his method and putting them to a somewhat different use.

Nozick is frequently referred to as a libertarian. This is now a label given to a brand of right wing theory that advocates individual freedom, the virtues of unregulated free markets and a radically diminished role for the state. It is an ideology associated with the right wings of the British Conservative and American Republican parties. However, as Haworth (1994) has suggested, this ideology is better described as *antilibertarianism* in that, despite its purported championing of individual freedom, it can only countenance one particular framework. Thus it presents the contradiction of deterministic outcomes — the citizen *must* be free of regulation and the dead hand of the state — within a purportedly non-deterministic ideology. Moreover this form of so-called libertarianism is frequently (and preversely) coupled with nationalism and social authoritarianism. Haworth places Nozick in this tradition. His sees Nozick, particularly as a result of his work, *Anarchy, State and Utopia*, as being one of the principle ideologues and architects of the libertarian right.

However, such a view oversimplifies Nozick's work. Whilst Nozick would certainly appear to be on the right of the spectrum in terms of the views on equality and distribution, other aspects of his libertarianism, such as his defence of animal rights, put him in the company of many on the left. The point here is that his libertarianism is consistent across the economic, moral and social spheres. Thus Nozick's ideas are more consistent than that associated with the libertarian right with its links with nationalism and social authoritarianism. This is because Nozick is more rigorous in his rejection of determinism. Whilst this does lead him to reject such notions as social justice and redistribution, it does separate Nozick from the antilibertarians described by Haworth. This non-determinism, or anti-essentialism, is what will be of use to me in developing a suitable method for housing studies.

As Wolff (1991) points out in his critique of Nozick, this label of libertarianism was once seen as referring to a brand of socialism that rejected the statism and authoritarianism of marxism and fabianism. Indeed there has been a libertarian tradition in housing and planning that dates from the work of Howard and Geddes in the 19th Century to Goodman and Segal and onto the more recent work of Birchall (1988), Ospina (1987), Turner (1972; 1976) and Ward (1985, 1990) (for a discussion of this tradition see Ward, 1991). This essay will have more in common with the outcomes suggested by these writers than with Nozick's *Anarchy, State and Utopia*. However, the element I seek to use in Nozick is precisely his concern for the moral rectitude of processes rather than any particular outcome. Thus I feel able to use elements of Nozick's method, and combine them with other insights, without accepting all of his starting assumptions.

Nozick has developed a method that recognises that philosophical structures are but temporary and that, as a result, a more contingent, pluralistic approach is called for. Nozick describes his approach by using the metaphor of two diverse architectural structures. He describes the traditional approach based upon proof and refutation:

Philosophers often seek to deduce their total view from a few basic principles, showing how all follows from their intuitively based axioms. The rest of the philosophy then strikes readers as depending upon these principles. One brick is piled upon another to produce a tall philosophical tower, one brick wide. When the bottom brick crumbles or is removed, all topples, burying even those insights that were independent of the starting point. (1981, p.3)

Traditional philosophy is here depicted as an unstable tower which, whatever its adornments, has foundations no wider than itself. If these foundations are found wanting then the entire philosophical edifice collapses. Nozick sees this situation as symptomatic of "coercive philosophy" (1981, p.4) which is based on proof and refutation. It is a concern with placing one brick on another, inexorably and logically, to create a direct line to truth. The structure can brook no alternative or divergence. It is all or nothing, and thus if it crumbles there is nothing left but a mess of broken hypotheses and theories.

Coercive philosophy is based upon *argument*; on building up one's tower whilst trying to knock down those of one's opponents. One wins because of the force and power of one's arguments. Nozick notes that the language of argument is violent and confrontational. He questions whether this is in any sense a useful procedure. Not only is it unpleasant to force a person into a particular position, it is morally deficient: "a person is not improved by being forced to believe something against his will" (1981, p. 5). In addition, there is no necessary relation between the force of an argument and truth:

Does either the likelihood of arriving at a true view (as opposed to a consistent and coherent one) or a view's closeness to the truth vary directly with the strength of philosophical arguments? (1981, p.5)

To adopt such a view is continually to believe that human perfectibility has been attained with the latest, and thereby the strongest philosophical argument. It is continually to state that each new argument is the end of philosophical debate. The very frequency of this claim throughout the history of philosophy shows its paucity.

Nozick therefore goes on to introduce an alternative formulation for philosophy seen metaphorically not as a tower, but as the Parthenon, where philosophers:

> ... emplace our separate philosophical insights column by column; afterwards, we unite and unify them under an overarching roof of general principles or themes. When the philosophical structure crumbles somewhat, as we should expect on inductive grounds, something of interest and beauty remains standing. Still preserved are some insights, the separate columns, some balanced relations, and the wistful look of a grander unity eroded by misfortunes or natural processes. (1981, p.3)

This picture is one of diverse concepts and hypotheses mutually supporting general principles. Yet these principles are not solely dependent upon one foundation, nor are the foundations themselves mutually dependent. Thus when the intellectual earthquake strikes, some of the structure may be damaged, but all is not lost. There are still some usable structures, either just the columns or perhaps some of the overarching beams as well.

Nozick calls this method *philosophical explanation*. It is a concern not with whether something is true or not, but with attempts at understanding how something is or can be possible. Certain explanations may be nearer to the truth than others, but even palpably false hypotheses may offer enlightenment and valuable insight. These insights would have to be foregone if proof and refutation were the sole criterion for philosophical enquiry.

Proof and refutation is thus of limited use. As a method it does not inform us whether a certain thing can be true: "(a) proof of p will give us the conviction that p is true, but it need not give us understanding of how p can be true" (1981, p. 10). The process of proving that the hypothetical unit p is true is a circular one. It is already believed that p is true and therefore it takes the argument no further.

But to concentrate upon explanation is to allow one to understand how p can be true and therefore how things may fit together in the world. Explanation is thus about heightening understanding. Instead of proof and refutation it is an attempt to describe and account for the world. As Nozick's metaphor of the Parthenon implied, it is also a method that is pluralist. It accepts diversity and opposition without trying to refute and counter it. Fundamentally it is a view that respects these opposing views sufficiently to want to learn from them. One does not have to accept an idea in its totality and reject all others in order to see merit in applying aspects of it, along with other ideas that one may have come across.

Philosophy and the development of ideas should be pluralistic. There are a large number of different mutually incompatible philosophical theories. Many of these have merits, though they could not possibly be put together as a consistent whole. Nozick sees that such an attempt at consistency is not necessary. Philosophy should rather be concerned with possibility: "(t)he major philosophical theories of continuing interest are readings of possible worlds accessible from here, that is, possible readings of the actual world" (1981, p. 21). If philosophy is concerned with how the world is, it will thus be both messy and inconclusive.

Nozick thus offers two insights for the purposes of developing a libertarian methodology of description: firstly, that coercive arguments are deficient, both morally and intellectually; secondly, explanation and understanding should supplant proof and refutation as methodological tools. In this way it will be possible to describe the world as it appears to individuals in their particular context, rather than trying merely to identify the world with a particular argument about its nature.

Such a method can help us to concentrate on what housing does — on understanding its place as a thing in the world that households are attached to and help to create through a series of diverse processes.

I have claimed that Nozick's methodology is a libertarian one and this is particularly pronounced when he expounds his non-patterned principle in his most famous work, *Anarchy, State and Utopia* (1974). This is a work, which starts from the premise that individual rights are inviolable, that seeks to show that the only state consistent with such rights is the libertarian minimal state. Nozick describes a non-teleological process by which, through a need to protect their rights, individuals voluntarily come together into mutually protective agencies which eventually combine into a monopoly protective agency. There are problems with Nozick's conception of the minimal state, particularly his defence of human rationality and his starting point that depends on the existence of natural rights, but the primary concern at present is the importance he gives to this non-teleological or *non-patterned* development of the minimal state. He states that there is no pattern or end-state principle of justice that determines the development and continued maintenance of the state.

A patterned principle is one that prescribes the form of distribution or prejudges outcomes within a society. Thus it is where a particular distribution of resources is seen as just. However, Nozick believes that such a situation is by definition morally unjust as it imposes a particular pattern, and thus it infers continual interference in people's lives in order to realise that pattern of distribution.

The importance of the non-patterned principle to our discussion, however, is not that it supports his view of the minimal state, but rather that it reinforces plurality. There can be no predetermined purpose or pattern to a state or a community. Rather a community develops out of voluntary association around the practice of living. There are no necessary outcomes for a particular community, rather only possibilities. One may personally determine something as just or unjust, but this implies no greater status to that position than that held by another.

Thus a reading of Nozick's work allows us to present both a methodology and a principle that are pluralistic and anti-essentialist. They do not predispose us towards a particular outcome or universal condition. Of course, the acceptance of this method does not imply agreement with all of Nozick's hypotheses. I shall rather make use of those parts seen as significant and useful to my purposes without accepting the implications of his natural rights argument that leads to a minimal state. I shall also feel free, as Nozick himself suggests, to place his ideas alongside those of others who may be seen as antithetical. This is necessary inorder to weaken Nozick's notion of philosophical explanation, without destroying the principal virtues.

Whilst Nozick's method aims to provide for greater pluralism, his use of the term "explanation" carries with it the connotation of being definitive, namely, that a problem has *an* explanation. Thus there is still an implication within Nozick's concept of reductionism, whereas one would expect an anti-essentialist concept to maximise possibilities. Therefore I seek to weaken the concept of philosophical explanation to that of *philosophical description.* Such a concept would recognise the incommensurability of diverse ideas, but use their salient elements to attempt to describe possibilities that may be open to institutions, collectivities and individuals. This is what Rorty (1980) describes as "edifying philosophy". This is philosophy as a method of dialogue, which is non-coercive. As Rorty describes it, it is "to decry the very notion of having a view while avoiding having a view about having views" (1980, p. 371). If all there is is a multiplicity of diverse and incommensurable views on the world then all we can do is engage with them and encourage a dialogue between them. There is not one view that underpins all others to which we can have recourse to and seek to supplant above them.

Thus instead of proof and refutation edifying philosophers offer therapy and description. It is not the role of edifying philosophers to peddle a particular view or argument, but rather to become involved in a conversation that opens up the possibility of further dialogue and assists others in the development of their positions. The role of the edifying philosopher is that of participant and facilitator, but one who cannot be expected to have any answers.

Thus philosophical description is where the philosopher enters into a dialogue through the description of various concepts, histories, ideas and theories inorder to allow others to define and refine their opportunities for self creation. It is a method that rejects any attempt to create rigid typologies (e.g. Somerville, 1994) because, no matter how useful these may be, they serve only to artificially circumscribe discourse. Instead of attempting to delimit a discourse by locating its ontological and epistemological essence, philosophical description recognises that commensurability within discourse is a consequence of perception. The significance of any description is therefore in its reception.

Philosophical description is open to the critique that it is not a critical method, in that it appears that it is not whether a description is correct or valid that is seen as significant, but rather it is perceived. It could be suggested therefore that it does not matter whether a description is patently false. However, in discussing the effect of Modern Conservative ideology I shall note that it is indeed the way a discourse is perceived rather than its objective validity that is significant. Modern Conservative consists of two "objectively" contradictory discourses that are able to coexist because of the significance both elements give to the notion of housing-as-property. Neither of these discourses have to be necessarily true in order for them to create the resignification of housing.

Philosophical description is not therefore an uncritical method, but rather one that is critical in a particular sense. It is not critical in the sense of determining coherence, but rather in the deconstructive sense of developing an understanding of the aporetic nature of discourses themselves (Derrida, 1976, Critchley, 1992). It is a method that seeks to understand a discourse from within its own boundaries and thus to appreciate why it is perceived as significant.

This, of course, places limitations on the procedures I may use in this undertaking. Nor is philosophical description a method that could be applicable to all the legitimate concerns within the diverse field of housing studies. It should be seen merely as one possible method open to housing researchers. Its usefulness does not denigrate the applicability of other methods, either with regard to the issues discussed in this essay or other areas of research. Nor should philosophical description be rejected merely because it does not find favour with other researchers. There is no reason to suggest that there can only be one way of carrying out research. The *art* of housing studies is therefore to find a method best suited to the problem faced by the researcher.

Thus philosophical description is a limited and limiting method. It is therefore likely to be useful in this analysis of the limits of housing policy. The next task is to begin this description by a critique of the nature of modernist housing policy. Having done this I shall then be able to begin to weave together a possible description for anti-essentialist, non-patterned housing policies which respects their limits.

CHAPTER TWO

MODERNIST HOUSING POLICY

2.1. Modern Conservatism

I have identified a number of concerns arising from the exclusive concentration on the provision of dwelling units and the consequent disregard of the uses to which these units may be put. Furthermore I have stated that the concept of housing more often refers to a commodity than to a process. Housing is perceived as the physical aggregate of dwelling structures. Such a situation serves to neglect the significance of housing as the process that facilitates human dwelling.

If we are to understand this neglect we need to identify what it is within current housing policy that allows for the commodification of housing. I believe the most useful way of pursuing this is not through a historical study, but by a description of the ideology that informs policy. My interest is in the purposes to which policy seeks to fulfil and not its development over time. As there have only been Conservative governments since 1979 I shall concentrate on recent conservative political ideology to try and establish a purpose for the policies pursued. However, though I shall concentrate on conservatism, I do so only because they are as typical of modernity as those that preceded them. Like the post war Labour government, they have attempted to impose a total policy as if there can be no possibility of a tenable alternative.

I shall refer to the Thatcher and Major administrations and their supporters as the Modern Conservatives and it is important to make clear why. There are three reasons why I have done so. Firstly, despite the strong strands of continuity, the result of the 1979 election led to a distinctly different strand of "conservatism-in-action" gaining control of political power. This election saw the empowerment of a positivist and activist approach to government. It could not be characterised as traditionalist and merely reactive, secure only in its natural right to govern. This was rather a government with a particular purpose beyond its own continuation in office. Its aim was to radically change the political landscape and reform the institutions and political culture of Britain. Thus it is possible to differentiate between traditional conservatism and the purposive post-1979 Modern Conservatives.

Secondly, this activism and positivism can be seen as typical of the modern project. The Thatcher and Major administrations have had a specific purpose which has seen them actively intervening in the lives of individuals. They have had a universalist perspective that could conceive of no alternative route because of the particular metaphysical foundation that supported their ideology. Thus the Thatcher and Major administrations can be portrayed as being "Modern" as distinct from pre- or postmodern. This identification is made explicit in the term "Modern Conservatism".

Thirdly, conservative writers such as Willets (1992) themselves make a distinction between the traditional and the modern. Willets believes that the Conservative party was forced into re-presenting itself to the electorate in response to the success of the Labour party in the 1945 election. This election appeared to be a major turning point in relations between government and electorate in terms of the latter's expectations of the role of politicians. A greater degree of intervention into both the public and private life was expected from government. If the Conservative party were to regain power they had to adapt into a more populist party in cognisance of the changed expectations of the electorate. Thus Willets suggests that the Conservative party modernised itself, taking on the same activist and interventionist role as the Labour party. Whilst the political objectives of the two parties may have remained distinct, and indeed diverged further after 1975, both of them have used the techniques of intervention and the centralisation of power in order to achieve their objectives. This means that one can date Modern Conservatism prior to 1979. However, one can equally state the post-1979 Conservatives created a distinctive project that diverged from the post war consensus. It was a distinctive form of modernity that broke with the corporatism adopted by both major political parties in Britain between 1945 and 1979.

It is therefore not my intention to suggest that there is no connection between the Modern Conservatives and traditional conservatism. The shift towards the modern was an evolutionary, rather than revolutionary one. The ideological climate already existed prior to Thatcher's election to the Conservative Party leadership in 1975. This election was merely part of the process of modernity rather than its point of ignition. The term "Modern Conservatism" has been chosen in preference to terms such as "Thatcherism" or "New Right" in order to show this evolutionary development out of the British conservative tradition as well as to emphasise the link with modernity. Regardless of their modernity, they are still conservatives with a particular set of traditions to appeal to that are specific and linked historically to the British political tradition. It is important to give due regard to this tradition of conservatism, which terms such as New Right (which explicitly references novelty and departure from the past) and Thatcherism (with its cult of the personality) fail to do sufficiently.

This referencing with the British Conservative tradition does not mean that Modern Conservatism is totally unrelated to developments in Europe and the USA. There are many ideological links between the Modern Conservatives and the American Republicans under Reagan, Bush and Gingrich. Indeed in certain respects there is a shared agenda between the right in Britain and the USA with their concern for the market and the re-moralisation of individuals through the reduction of state intervention (Adonis & Hames, 1994; Levitas, 1986a). Likewise there are links with developments in countries such as the Netherlands and Germany, particularly the withdrawal of subsidy to low income housing and the increasing emphasis on owner occupation and private sector solutions (Priemus, 1995).

These links are to be expected because of the very totalising nature of modernity. Whilst it is undoubtedly the case that many national peculiarities have been maintained, modernist ideology and its consequent means of provision have created a considerable overlap of policy outcomes across the western world and increasingly into the developing world. Modernity, particularly in architecture and planning has been a truly international phenomena, and in many ways it is in its physical manifestations that modernity's attempt to universalise is most obvious.

2.2 Commodification

The essential element of Modern Conservative ideology is the centrality of the role of private property rights as a determinant in creating a social order that rewards individual moral responsibility and decision making. Thus a primary effect of this ideology has been the commodification of housing whereby its significance is determined by its economic value and its currency within a market.

However, to concentrate on Modern Conservative ideology begs the question of whether the commodification of housing existed prior to 1979. The answer, of course, is that it did, but to a lesser extent and, crucially, without being the primary aim of policy. Indeed the private provision of housing has predominated throughout human history and is still the norm for the majority of the world's population (Ward, 1990). However, private provision is not the sole prerequisite for commodification. For this to occur the production and consumption of housing needs to be monetised (Rose, 1989) which is not the case for those living a subsistence existence. Commodification needs a market allowing for the voluntary exchange of goods and services.

Markets for housing, to rent and to own, obviously predate 1979 and indeed private ownership was the majority tenure before Thatcher's election. Moreover, because it is possible to exclude others from the benefits of one's housing, a market for it has always been possible in a way that is not the case with education and health care. The identification of property rights in housing has allowed it to be readily commodified notwithstanding the particular ideological propensities of the Thatcher and Major governments. Forrest and Murie (1988) have shown that post-war governments of both political parties have encouraged owner occupation as a tenure and that even the Attlee government saw it as desirable in itself. Indeed owner occupation and the tradability of housing has become increasingly important over the post-war period (Daunton, 1987). Thus commodification existed as a phenomenon before 1979.

What does differentiate the post-1979 period is the explicit nature of the government's encouragement of owner occupation, the exclusivity of policy and the emphasis of the role of markets in achieving it. Previous governments may have encouraged owner occupation, but not with the vigour and single-mindedness of the Modern Conservatives, whereby even policy aimed at reforming other tenures is intended to have a beneficial effect on owner occupation. Therefore it is the extent to which the Modern Conservatives have championed both ownership and the benefits of the market that sets them apart from their predecessors. Forrest and Murie (1988) are correct to identify the monetarist squeeze on the public sector and the heightened emphasis on private sector solutions to allocative problems as beginning several years before 1979. However, such a trend was as a result of a reluctant recognition of the consequences of economic decline rather than because of ideological zeal or conviction.

The extension of ownership has rather been one of the central goals of the Modern Conservatives' programme for government. It has shifted away from the post war consensus of balancing individual economic freedom with the social objectives of extending equality, and moved towards the promotion of private ownership as the means of fulfilment. As Gamble (1988) has stated:

> A central goal has been to discredit the social democratic concept of universal citizenship rights, guaranteed and enforced through public agencies and to replace it with a concept of citizenship rights achieved through property ownership and participation in markets. (1988, p.16)

The social democracy practised by previous governments did not denigrate private ownership, but rather saw the need to balance it, and to mitigate some of its excesses, with a strong public sector. The essential difference precipitated by the 1979 election was the tilting of this balance in the direction of private provision.

Thus whilst housing was commodified to an extent prior to 1979, after this date it became central to the programme of the government. Indeed this commodification of housing can be seen as being the inevitable corollary of private ownership. This is because of the linkage between private property and the market through which we are able to acquire and voluntarily dispose of that which we own. We are thus defined, through our relation to the market and to property. Our part in society is obtained and ultimately circumscribed by our accumulation of commodities. Our most significant acts occur in our roles as consumers and therefore housing has a meaning for us as a commodity. Furthermore its use is determined by the access it allows into markets as a means of exchange. It is not the nature of property relations that have altered under the Modern Conservatives, but rather the meanings that are attached to these relations.

Therefore there is considerable justification in concentrating on Modern Conservative ideology, which, whilst not founding commodification, has created the intellectual legitimisation enabling a shift in the balance between tenures and the attribution of new meanings to them. This has occurred to the extent that housing is now primarily seen as a tradable commodity with a value as opposed to an intrinsic use. Housing now has meaning as the desire for the ownership of property.

2.3. Modern Conservative Housing Policy

Although the Conservative Party was elected in 1979 on an agenda of radical political change, it was not until after the 1987 General election that they undertook a major reform of housing provision. A number of earlier innovations were introduced, in particular the Right-to-Buy and the Tenants' Charter, but these were all within the context of the existing structures of provision. Whilst the effects of these innovations should not be discounted, the Modern Conservatives accepted the central role of local authorities and public subsidy in the provision of housing. Indeed more generally, the Welfare State had survived relatively intact up until the third term of the Thatcher government. However, following the 1987 election the government turned its attention to the reform of three major areas of public provision, namely, the National Health Service, comprehensive education and public housing.

The reasons why the Modern Conservatives waited until their third term are perhaps not immediately obvious. It may have been that they felt that the reform of these major public institutions, particularly the health service, could only be undertaken in an incrementalist fashion because of bureaucratic and organisational inertia, political opposition and public opinion. They thus had to prepare the political ground by years of restraint in public spending and an antithetical rhetoric towards public provision and institutions. They may have felt that the electorate were not ready to accept radical changes to public institutions prior to 1987 and therefore a period of "softening up" was necessary.

However, the result of the 1987 election, fought on a more overtly ideological agenda than in 1983, against a more organised and credible opposition and after 8 years in which the electorate were able to judge the attractiveness of the Modern Conservative ideology, showed that the electorate were prepared to accept a free market version of conservatism. The Modern Conservatives could state this as being the case regardless of the "real" reasons for being returned to office. Even if the majority of electors voted for the Conservative Party out of fear of the Labour Party, this still showed a preference of sorts for the Modern Conservative political agenda over its competitors. Election victory, because the process is generally accepted, gave legitimacy to the victors, who could then claim that they had a mandate to review and re-organise housing provision along market oriented lines. Again the perception of events is important, although on this occasion it is the perceptions of the players within the political process itself rather than the recipients of policy.

Thus in September 1987 the government published the White Paper, "Housing: The Government's Proposals" (DOE, 1987) with the aim of reforming housing legislation in England and Wales. The government claimed that it had four main aims:

> Firstly, to reverse the decline of private rented housing and to improve its quality; second, to give council tenants the right to transfer to other landlords if they choose to do so; third, to target money more accurately on the most acute problems; and fourth, to continue to encourage the growth of home ownership. (1987, p.1)

Whilst the post-war consensus approach to housing policy had attempted to modify the quality, quantity, price, and ownership and control of dwellings (Malpass and Murie, 1990), the government's housing policy was now to show an exclusive concern with the owner-ship and control of dwellings. There was a belief that the most beneficial levels of quality, quantity and price — the major deter-minants of supply and demand — would flow from the correct modes of ownership.

The government believed that one group of owners (private landlords) was being unfairly restrained; another group (owner occupiers) was in continued need of encouragement; whilst a third group (local authorities) were delivering a poor service and were thus frustrating the desires and ambitions of their tenants. Thus the White Paper states:

> Too much pre-occupation since the war with controls in the private rented sector, and mass provision in the public rented sector, has resulted in substantial numbers of rented houses and flats which are badly designed and maintained and which fail to provide decent homes. The return to private sector landlords has been inadequate to persuade them to stay in the market or to keep their property in repair. In the public sector too little attention has been paid to the wishes of tenants or their views on how their requirements can best be met; tenants have generally not been allowed to express their choices clearly and have therefore not always found the kind of accommoda-tion they want. In the worst cases this has led to understandable resentment and a consequent lack of commitment to their homes. (DOE, p.1)

With regard to owner occupation the White Paper stated:

> Clearly, the majority of people wish to own their own homes. This wish should, in the Government's view, be supported. Home ownership gives people independence; it gives them a sense of greater personal responsibility: and it helps to spread the Nation's wealth more widely. These are important factors in the creation of a more stable and prosperous society, and they justify the favourable tax treatment accorded to borrowing for house pur-chase by owner occupiers. (1987, p.2)

Thus the government believed that by altering ownership and property rights it could revitalise the system of housing provision. The White

Paper went on to identify how this was to be achieved.

The government aimed to reverse the decline in the private rented sector. It felt that private landlords were disinclined to reinvest or remain in the sector because of rent control and the security of tenure enjoyed by tenants. Landlords were unable either to obtain a return related to their costs, or to enter and leave the market according to their own choosing. Therefore the government aimed to remove controlled rents and to limit security of tenure in all new private sector tenancies. These new contractual tenancies, either assured or assured shorthold, were to be at market rents with enhanced, and indeed in certain cases mandatory grounds for possession.

Infact the government aimed to create what it termed the "Independent Rented Sector" (p. 9) by amalgamating the private rented sector with the voluntary housing movement. Housing association tenants had benefited from the same regime of rent control and security of tenure as those in the private sector, but with the advantage of relatively high quality new build or rehabilitated accommodation. All new housing association tenants would henceforth experience the same contractual rights as those in the private sector.

Housing associations were to be seen as central to the government's proposals. It was planned to expand the role of housing associations into the major providers of social rented housing (p. 19). However, this planned expansion was to be driven by an injection of private funding rather than solely through public finance. Housing Association Grant would be predetermined rather than being set at the end of the development process according to the rent level and the housing association's running costs for the scheme. The difference between this fixed grant level and the cost of the development was to be funded from private sector loans. This was why new tenants would lose their statutory rights and, where applicable, their Right-to Buy. It was felt that landlords would need to convince the financial markets of their ability to control and manage their stock. This ability would be enhanced by assured tenancies at market rents set by the association itself rather than the independent Rent Officer.

Housing associations were envisaged as being the major providers of new social housing. Yet this was to be achieved without an increase in public subsidy. The expansion was to be funded through private finance. The consequence of this was to open up the provision of housing association dwellings to the disciplines of economic markets. Associations would have to convince financial institutions of their viability to repay a commercial loan. Furthermore the limiting of public funding would lead to increasing levels of competition between associations.

The government's reasons for expanding the housing association sector appear, at least partially, to be negative ones. Associations, unlike local authorities, are free of political control and thus not vulnerable to the swings of the electoral process. They do not have recourse to an alternative store of political legitimacy which may lead them to pursue policies against the government's interests. Furthermore, associations are generally smaller than local authorities in terms of units in management, with only 117 registered associations managing more than 1,000 dwellings in 1988 (Langstaff, 1988). They were thus taken to be less prone to bureaucracy and inaccessibility which were seen by the Modern Conservatives as being typical of local authorities. The government therefore turned to housing associations as its primary vehicle for new public provision largely because of their antipathy towards local authorities. In addition however, housing associations, because of their size, unity of function and historical dependence on central government subsidy, are more controllable than the larger, politically autonomous local authorities.

The White Paper's principal concern with control was shown especially by its plans for the local authority sector. The White Paper describes the quality of life on too many estates as being unsatisfactory, and as places where tenants would not live from choice. The assumption was that council tenants would leave the sector at the earliest opportunity. This, of course, ignores the apparent contradiction of over one million tenants "leaving" the sector through purchasing the property they were currently living in on the very same estate (Forrest and Murie, 1988).

Despite this existing indication of tenants' preferences the White Paper proposed to introduce "Tenant's Choice" (p.15) whereby tenants would be able to opt out of local authority control and turn instead to a private landlord, housing association, or by establishing a co-operative to manage their accommodation. In addition the government proposed to transfer the ownership of certain rundown estates to Housing Action Trusts which would rehabilitate the stock using a mixture of public and private funding and then transfer it into the private sector.

These proposals were enacted in two stages in the form of the Housing Act 1988 and Local Government and Housing Act 1989. The first act sought to restructure the housing association and private sectors, through the introduction of contractual tenancies, the limiting of Housing Association Grant, Tenants' Choice giving local authority tenants the right to choose an alternative landlord, and Housing Action Trusts to inject private sector funding into the worst local authority estates. The Housing Act 1988 can be seen as having two main purposes. Firstly it offered opportunities and incentives to a number of groups. It sought to give housing associations more freedom in terms of rent setting and income generation. The act aimed to give private landlords an incentive to remain in this sector and in the long term to encourage its expansion. It also sought to give local authorities tenants the possibility of changing their landlord to one more amenable to their needs. Whilst these renewed opportunities played an important part in the government's rhetoric, one could perhaps say that the major purpose of the act was to put in place a structure of provision suited to the government's vision for housing provision. It sought a transference of the major responsibility for rented housing from local authorities to housing associations and the private sector. In doing so it sought to open up rented housing to a market through the use of private finance by associations and by reducing statutory restrictions on rent levels. This situation should be seen in terms of the rhetoric favouring owner occupation. This was seen as the main, or "normal", tenure with only a residual safety net of public housing being necessary for those unable to attain to ownership. Housing associations were seen as the organisations to provide this safety net rather than local authorities. However, because of the reforms to housing association finance, they were to be much more commercially oriented. Thus all forms of housing provision were to be placed within the framework of a market.

The Local Government and Housing Act 1989 established a new financial regime for local authorities. As well as restructuring urban renewal provision, the act introduced changes both to capital and revenue funding. In terms of capital finance it tightened the government's control by restricting the use of capital receipts and by taking them into account when determining credit approvals. It also closed several loopholes which allowed local authorities to circumvent the government's spending restrictions. The revenue changes included the introduction of capital value rents which were intended to relate local authority rents to local property values Secondly, the act ring fenced each authorities housing revenue account (HRA). The effect of this was prohibit the subsidisation of either the HRA or the General Fund. Thirdly, the various subsidies to the HRA were amalgamated which, because of the dependence of a majority of tenants on housing benefit, gave the government further control over local rent levels and total spending. These financial reforms considerably restricted the ability of local authorities to fulfil their legal and contractual obligations, whilst at the same time increasing the cost of the service to tenants (Malpass et Al, 1993). The purpose of the Housing and Local Government Act 1989 can be seen as an attempt to make local authority housing less attractive as a tenure. The increase in rents, the reduction in services and the limitation on capital finance were seen as an attempt to push tenants to take up the opportunities open to them through the Housing Act 1988.

This legislation was concerned therefore with the various rented sectors. However, we can see these two pieces of legislation as being more concerned with a restructuring of the relations between renting and ownership. It was a part of the shift of resources from direct subsidy of new provision to support for dwellers. Moreover the large rent increases resulting from the legislation reduced the difference between the cost of renting and home ownership, as well as reducing the ability of local authorities to provide a comprehensive and enhanced service (Malpass et al, 1993; Malpass & Means, 1993). The intention of the legislation could therefore be seen as an attempt to reduce the desirability of renting, particularly in the local authority sector, with a view to pushing more tenants into owner occupation. The continuation of social housing was still envisaged, but under circumstances aimed at encouraging greater independence and control on the part of tenants and a reduced role for the state. We will show that the achieved outcomes were not as envisaged, largely because of the condition of the housing market in the early 1990s, and accordingly the government was forced into a series of ad hoc moves in order to protect home ownership as both a mass tenure and the major plank of the Modern Conservative housing discourse.

However, before I discuss this failure I need to describe the ideology which underpinned the reforms determined by the 1987 White Paper. I shall then attempt to make some assessment of the effects they have had on the perceived meanings given to housing and accordingly why the policies pursued were unsustainable.

2.4. The Role of Property

A significant difference between the Modern Conservative governments and their predecessors in the post war period has been their attitude towards the rights of citizens. The post war social democratic consensus highlighted the civil, social and political rights of members of society (Marshall, 1985). Policy, in housing as elsewhere, was determined by the objective of extending these rights. The nature of these rights highlighted the importance of the collective to the citizen, rather than focusing on the individual or household in isolation. There was thus a concentration on the creation and distribution of public goods and one could say that the rights of the citizen were defined in relation to access to these public goods.

The situation since 1979 has been markedly different. The Modern Conservative governments have been concerned with what has been termed the "property owning democracy" (Daunton, 1987; Jordan, 1989), where our membership of a society is defined in terms of access to, and possession of, private goods. It was felt that by linking asset distribution to citizenship, every citizen, by becoming a property owner, would share a common interest in the developing Modern Conservative social order (Jordan, 1989). Accordingly citizens should be encouraged into the ownership of property, in the form of shares in former public corporations and nationalised industries and, most significantly, in their own housing.

The Modern Conservatives have equated private property with home ownership in a very explicit sense. Owning one's own home is a ready possibility for the majority of citizens who are in secure employment. The availability of long term finance and government subsidy through tax relief and exemptions and discounts for certain public sector tenants made it even more possible for households on moderate and low incomes. In this way housing became to be seen much more as a private good with its elemental qualities for security, personal identification and orientation becoming equated to an economic rather than an existential significance. The political purpose of the Modern Conservatives can thus be seen as the attempt to heighten the economic significance of housing as a private good.

Jordan defines the "property owning democracy" when he states that:

> What the phrase implies is that (Mrs Thatcher's) form of democracy consists in extending these property rights as widely as possible because they represent a stake in a market-based system. (1989, p.98)

Citizenship, as a form of social cohesion and belonging, is defined through the relation to personal private property. It links individual citizens to the collective through the actions of individuals themselves, rather than through the state acting on behalf of the collective.

Already the link between Modern Conservative's defining ideological characteristics are becoming clear. Citizenship rights encapsulate freedom and liberty to individual action in a market and are enhanced and given expression through property rights. Firstly, therefore, we need to understand the nature of property ownership and how it links into the Modern Conservative's housing policy.

Between 1979 and 1992 owner-occupation in Britain increased from 55% of households to 68%. It is thus the form of tenure experienced by over two-thirds of households. It could therefore be termed the "normal" tenure, in the sense of it forming the basis for the majority's expectations with regard to their housing.

In as much as council housing is seen as state housing, owner-occupation is perceived as being privatised. As a result it is deemed to enhance independence and individual choice. We have already seen that this presumption in the government's White Paper (DOE, 1987). In the public sector choice is circumscribed and determined by others. Furthermore, households are described as having only a restricted amount of independence. In this context owner-occupation is seen as way of freeing oneself from this circumscription imposed by the state.

Yet as Forrest and Murie have pointed out:

> The owner-occupied sector has become a state sponsored, subsidised sector rather than a deregulated private sector. (1988, p.234)

Indeed during a prolonged period of public sector restraint the Modern Conservatives maintained a system of tax relief to mortgages that has been relatively open ended and, until 1990 favoured those with higher incomes by allowing tax relief to be claimed at the highest rate of tax paid by the mortgagee. It was only in 1994, when the public finances were in severe deficit and with social housing spending apparently pared down to an absolute minimum, that mortgage interest tax relief was reduced.

Thus despite a rhetoric of privatism the reality is that of government encouragement on both the political and financial level. The White Paper is quite explicit in this regard when it states that to maintain a high level of government financial support is justified, whilst the opposite apparently applies in the case of housing associations (DOE, 1987). There is then a breach between the rhetoric and the reality, which is perhaps unsurprising considering the complexity of intervening at the level of national provision. It is however indicative of the fact that political practice operates on at least two levels. Firstly, we can observe the rhetorical, exhortative expressive level of public statements, white papers, speeches and the like. This is where ideology is expressed — sometimes openly, at other times obliquely — in order to create or modify the perceptions of the listeners. Secondly, there is the sphere of action, where rhetoric meets the realities of government in the sense of competing financial and physical resources, bureaucratic inertia, the influence of pressure groups and other interests, and of course, the need for periodic re-election.

This leads into a general, but nevertheless interesting side issue. If ideology is tempered, modified and moderated by the reality of political action, should we really be considering it as the focus of policy? Should we not rather see Modern Conservative ideology as no more than a veneer of rhetoric over the traditional positional type of conservatism apparently concerned with governance for its own sake to maintain the social order (Gamble, 1988). Indeed conservative writers such as Boyson (1978) and Scruton (1980) have emphasised the essentially pragmatic view of conservative government as the maintenance, or conservation, of the social order. It does not necessarily believe in a particular set of discrete aims as such. For the conservative, government, according to Honderich (1990), is concerned with the pursuit and attainment of extrinsic rather than intrinsic rewards.

The position that conservatives are merely concerned with the conservation of the social order, however, begs a rather obvious question. It presumes the existence or possibility of a given social order that is worth conserving. Conservatives must therefore have some normative vision of what it is within a society that is to be defended. Such a vision is the realm of ideology as a vehicle for the forming of perceptions of the Good. Thus, even if we accept the view of Boyson and Scruton that conservatism is about governance, this still implies a particular ideological framework, for otherwise conservatives would be happy to conserve any social order. This suggests that the conservative view of government is infact purposive. It does have a set of discrete aims, in that a particular vision of the social order is to be defended. Thus it is not government for its own sake, but rather government that it as ideological as any other.

The debate about the meaning of Thatcherism, or indeed whether such a thing exists or existed, has been discussed at length and with a frustrating lack of conclusiveness (see in particular Skidelsky, 1988 and Gamble, 1988). However, there is a view that suggests that there was no real coherence to Thatcherism. Commentators such as Riddell have attempted to show that the constraints were so tight on policy making that outcomes were often uncertain and unattainable (discussed in Gamble, 1988). There was thus considerably more continuity with previous administrations than there were differences.

Furthermore it has been suggested that political action is largely a reaction to circumstance and that ideology is thus relatively unimportant:

> ... politics, as politicians well know is largely a matter of giving names to what is happening anyway and persuading people to vote for it. (Hollis, quoted in Gamble, 1988, p.202)

This idea of government reacting to circumstance has been taken up by Hindess (1987). He states that whilst a government may enact legislation, it in effect can often do no more than cajole, encourage, entreat or just hope that individuals, groups and enterprises act accordingly. No government is able to start from scratch, at least not in a democracy bound by some sense of a moral order. Instead a government must largely accept and work within the situation they have inherited:

> ... governments maintain the bulk of the activities and organisations they inherit, and they attempt to shift the balance in one direction or another. Governments are rarely able to introduce entirely new patterns of organisation or spending without considerable preparation beforehand. On the whole changes are introduced in an incremental fashion, leaving the greater part of the state machine intact. (Hindess 1987, p.95)

Hindess sees the role of any government as being limited by the weight of history, precedent and inertia, thus mitigating any single purpose.

We could therefore find support for the view that housing policy has been determined by factors rather more prosaic than high principle. We can view housing policy as the result of reactions to circumstance with principles being merely attached to action in retrospect.

Indeed these views have a certain credence to them, yet not to the extent of negating the position of ideology in policy making. The reality of political practice is such that politicians are constrained and they are often able to do no more than react to, or against, particular sets of circumstances. However, this is not a situation unique to the period following the 1979 election. The complexity of government and the reality of external constraint was as real in the period 1945-51 as in the post 1979 era. Yet we could not deny that a particular agenda, motivated by the ideology of social democracy, was implemented by the Attlee government. We can state that there was a discrepancy between intention and outcome, but not to the extent of disputing that a definite political shift occurred as a result of a particular ideological stance. Similarly we can view the post 1979 period as witnessing an ideologically motivated shift in public policy. Again there may be a deficit between the words of the politicians and the final outcomes, but this does not deny that a change did occur as a result of an ideological imperative.

There are several other points which can usefully be made here. Firstly, change may be said to occur because ideological statements are believed as being meaningful — they affect peoples' expectations. It would be churlish to deny that many politicians are sincere in the principles they espouse. Nor should we deny their skill and competence in presenting these principles. Equally their views are sincerely responded to by their supporters, their opponents and the electorate. Local politicians, for example, will alter their expectations and behaviour of what it is possible for them to achieve locally on the basis of what they believe central government is doing and what they believe it aims to do in the future. Thus by this token, Thatcherism exists because some people believe it does, because others believe in it, and because some people believe that others believe it does and believe in it!

Secondly, politicians develop their principles and beliefs long before they are able to exert power and influence. Fame may be the spur, but this does not tell us why an aspiring politician chose one party rather than another, especially in a political system that has seen power alternate thirteen times this century (a different point to the same effect is to question why people were prepared to join the Labour party in the mid 1980s and stand as candidates in elections when that party has not been in power since 1979. Why don't they become Conservative party members instead?).

Thirdly, the ideological background to policy is often developed outside of government. This was partially the case prior to 1945 (in party, if not totally in personnel) and was certainly so with the Modern Conservatives prior to 1979. Policy was thus developed free from the constraints of governance. Policy was often not forged in the heat of political action, but rather tempered by it subsequently.

Moreover, we should not ignore the influence of think tanks such as the Institute of Economic Affairs, the Adam Smith Institute and the Centre of Policy Studies, who are able to make policy free of the constraints of government, yet who have the ear of senior government members.

Finally, we can return to Hindess' quote to mitigate his position. He states that "(g)overnments are rarely able to introduce entirely new patterns of organisation or spending without considerable preparation beforehand" (1987, p.95). This implies that a government can make drastic changes only after a considerable period in office. This is precisely the case with the Modern Conservatives. As I have suggested the Modern Conservatives did not attempt to radically reform housing policy until after their third election victory. Indeed after their fourth election victory in 1992 the Modern Conservatives could have been even more sure of their political base, and of the divisions amongst their opponents. Whether the Modern Conservatives were elected for positive or negative reasons is in this case unimportant. What is crucial however is the belief, which certainly exists within the Conservative Party itself, that Modern Conservative ideology mirrors the views of the electorate. Thus there was a government which was increasingly able to combat inertia and resistance, and with the precedent of succeeding through ignoring its opponents. Put another way the opponents of the Modern Conservatives had no longer any reason to hope for a return to the social democratic consensus. Indeed, one can now reasonably suggest that the Modern Conservatives have created a "consensus" around their own ideological imperatives. They are thus now "able to introduce entirely new patterns of organisation" (Hindess, 1987, p.95) and indeed since 1987 have done so.

Therefore, despite the constraints and undoubted complications on government action, the role of ideology is significant. No one would seriously suggest that Britain's public institutions (erstwhile and remaining) would be in the same configuration now if the Labour party had remained in power after 1979. The realities of political practice impinge on policy, but not in a uniform way, and this is because of the effect of ideology.

As I have previously suggested, the perception of government for its own sake and of maintaining the social order is itself a manifestation of ideology. This perspective presupposes a particular attitude towards social institutions and social organisation that distinguishes it from other parties. As Scruton states:

> Conservatism arises directly from the sense that one belongs to some continuing and pre-existing social order, and this fact is all important in determining what to do. (1980, p.21)

It is, as it were, the ideology of non-ideological politics; an ideology of using the past as a guide to what to maintain for the future.

It is an ideal concerned with continuity, belonging and preservation rather than change and reform. The bedrock of this continuity and preservation, and what ties the citizen into society so that he or she belongs, is, as Scruton puts it, "man's absolute and ineradicable need for private property" (1980, p. 99). Ownership is seen as control, and because of its centrality it must be fought for against inertia and opposition. This need for property is non-negotiable. There can be no compromise over a need that cannot be eradicated. It is not the case then that ideology is tempered by reality, but rather reality is created out of the imperatives of ideology for, as I shall show, the reality of Modern Conservatism-in-power finds no contradiction in public action to further the private, often whilst maintaining a rhetoric hostile to public action.

It will be useful to pursue Scruton's description further to attempt to ascertain why property may be an absolute and ineradicable need. He states that the concern solely with the task of government cannot be translated into a set of social goals as such. The Modern Conservatives are not attempting to attain a specific programme, but are rather engaged in preserving what currently exists or in rediscovering the implicit nature of society. Such a view, as I have stated, refuses to acknowledge that there are ideological presumptions that underpin it such as inequality in wealth distribution and a particular social hierarchy, and as such is as goal orientated as other ideologies.

A Modern Conservative may well offer the rejoinder that they are aiming to preserve that which has developed implicitly over time through a non-planned social interaction, and that therefore they are not proposing a specific model of distribution and justice. But this presumes that they do not hold normative views on the particular patterns of distribution and justice taken as given within this society, for otherwise any currently existing social order would be worth defending simply because it is currently existing.

However, to return to Scruton's view, conservatives engage with "the surface of things" (1980, p.44); with, as we have stated above, extrinsic and not intrinsic rewards (Honderich, 1990). Humans, according to Scruton, only have rights over those things which they own. We only have a right to the permanent use of property. However, this is not an insubstantial right, as this is where stability is engendered within society — through the permanence of property and the right to its use. Scruton then sees humans as beings whose rationality is defined by property relations.

Scruton defines property in terms of an individual's right to the exclusive determination over certain objects in his or her legitimate possession. It is, as Ryan (1984) has suggested, a system of legal rules that recognise an individual's rights to use and transfer objects. Such a view is emphasised by Waldron (1988) who sees private property in terms of:

> rules laid down that, in the case of each object, the individual person whose name is attached to that object is to determine how the object shall be used and by whom. His decision is to be upheld by the society as final. (1988, p.39)

Thus it is the right of use upheld by law that defines property. This, of course, implies a duty or responsibility on other individuals and agencies within a society to recognise and respect these rights. Ownership of property should therefore be viewed in terms of rights and obligations — of exclusive use, exclusion and transfer — which become reified in the significance attached to these objects.

Ownership is the primary relation through which human beings and nature come together — it is how objects are socialised, controlled and brought into use. This essentially Lockean view is supplemented by a Kantian equation of freedom with rational action (Lindley, 1986). Scruton states that, "(t)hrough property man imbues his world with will, and begins therein to discover himself as a social being" (1980, p. 99). Without property we are unable to identify anything in the world as our own. We have no rights, merely desires and these, in the Kantian sense, do not equate to freedom or autonomy. Only through ownership do we lose these irrational desires and enter into a "state of self-consciousness" (p.99). Property rights enable us to view the world self-consciously in terms of our rights, responsibilities and freedoms. Property ownership is thus the path to self-realisation.

Moreover, property is perceived as the bonding of social relations. It forms the boundary of right and obligation within a society. It is the framework for responsible relations between citizens.

The moral justification for the centrality of property appears to be intuitive as Scruton offers no explanation as to why this state of affairs arises. Indeed Honderich (1990) points out that many of the arguments for property ownership are circular. Property ownership is a moral right for some because they have a moral right to property ownership. This, for Honderich, is akin to saying, "the society ought to be that way because that is the way it ought to be" (1990, p. 108). Property ownership is thus imbued with an almost mystical significance.

This perception of property rights is used and developed by Saunders in his work on home ownership (1990). He believes that there is a natural and deeply ingrained desire towards home ownership and that this is "an expression of a specific set of cultural values" (p.39). He feels that this can be shown by the similar tenure patterns of Britain and areas of British settlement such as New Zealand, Canada, Australia and the USA. Saunders believes that these tenure patterns derive from the traditional linkage between individualism and property ownership embedded in British culture. We find this echoed by Ryan (1987) in his discussion on the relation between property and political philosophy: "(m)odern freedom is the quiet enjoyment of private life" (p. 37). Individualism is defined negatively as non-interference with one's liberty and personal actions. Such freedom is best attained by maintaining the exclusivity of property.

Saunders goes on to suggest that humans are more prepared to commit themselves to that which they own and possess. He feels that we may have a deep desire to possess items exclusively to ourselves and this explains why humans are more likely to preserve that which they own, rather than that which they rent (1990, p.77). He contends that this is the general situation of human beings, but without going on to explain directly why individualism and ownership have developed into such a natural and deeply ingrained desire. Like Scruton, Saunders relies on intuitivism to bridge this void.

However, there is a more fundamental difficulty with Saunders' position. He is not able to suggest that the preservation of personal property is evidence of a deep desire amongst humans to possess as well as proposing that tenure patterns are similar in "British" cultures because of a specific set of cultural values. Either there is an immutable need for ownership or a set of cultural values that predispose certain communities to it, but both of these divergent explanations cannot exist side by side.

The notion that an innate possessiveness that leads us towards home ownership can be quickly dismissed merely by remembering how tenure patterns have changed in Britain since 1915 when private renting made up 89% of households. Moreover an international comparison of tenure patterns (which Saunders himself provides) leads us to speculate what has negated this innate desire in the Germans and the Swiss, who both are much less likely to be home owners. If there is an innate desire it has been sublimated by some more significant factor.

This factor may indeed be cultural and thus we might suggest that Saunders has uncovered a significant factor. However, again an analysis of international tenure patterns shows that Saunders will have problems in justifying even this. He suggests that the specific set of cultural values of British cultures derive from the linkage of individualism and property ownership. If this is the case we would expect nations without a tradition of individualism to have low levels of home ownership. However, according to Saunders' own data (p.19) two of the countries with the highest levels of home ownership are Bangladesh and the Philippines. Neither of these nations could be said to fit the Lockean model of liberal individualism.

Infact Saunders does mention elements of the reason for the preponderance of home ownership in Britain without getting to the essence of the matter. We may be able to accept that there are a set of cultural values, but this begs the question of how they are operationalised within the context of ideological reinforcement and referencing. The reason for the dominance of one tenure in Britain is because historically it has been reinforced by public action to the extent that it now carries with it various cultural references. As Saunders himself mentions, one of the major advantages of home ownership is financial, in that over a lifetime, *ceteris paribus*, it is cheaper to buy a property (and to gain an asset) than it is to rent. He is indeed more explicit:

> …home ownership is widely regarded as a secure form of investment which demands little attention, entails little risk and offers long-term substantial gains. (1990, p.20)

The desirability of home ownership may then derive from the likelihood of attaining financial gains rather than out of a deeply ingrained desire. The prospect and potential of financial benefits infuses into cultural values and alters perceptions at the common sense level. Thus the significant part of the above quote is the phrase, "widely regarded as". It is the perceptions and the resulting expectations of individuals that are crucial as the determinants of their actions. Home ownership has (until the early 1990s) been a good investment and has proved to be generally cheaper than renting and households have behaved accordingly.

This situation is further enhanced by the tax and other financial incentives offered to home owners by government. This returns us to the comment by Forrest and Murie regarding owner occupation as a state sponsored sector. Indeed Forrest and Murie see the supremacy of home ownership as being solely a pragmatic response to circumstance:

> ... it is clear that the current overwhelming preference for home

ownership is not natural, inherent or cultural but reflects the current realities of the stock of dwellings, the means of access to them, the way they are managed and the financial and policy framework. If and when these circumstances change, preferences will change. (1988, p.86)

Thus, according to Forrest and Murie, there is nothing intrinsic to property ownership.

However, this view, whilst interesting, is too simplistic. It neglects to take into account how the past creates expectations and thus alters behaviour. Individuals respond as their expectations change. They must perceive a change in circumstance and react accordingly, but within a particular given context. Of course, perceiving a change does not necessarily grant us the power to react sufficiently to it. Thus it is not just the financial and political context that creates a preference but the perceptions that households have towards them. Therefore, whilst agreeing that owner-occupation is neither natural or inherent, there is a cultural dimension as we cannot separate out particular elements from our culture. Moreover, cultural imperatives may operate to the effect that households perceive owner occupation to be natural and inherent.

Property, and more particularly home ownership is now fostered and supported by government. Government, of course, did not invent the tenure, nor is it particularly able to control its growth, but it has used owner occupation as a means to achieve and maintain the Modern Conservative social order. Property rights have been "recreated" with a new purpose in order to maintain what has been arrived at without design. The Modern Conservatives give no teleological explanation for the establishment of their social order, but this does not extend to the means of maintaining it.

Property rights are therefore at the centre of Modern Conservative ideology. This is because of two linked reasons. Firstly, the Modern Conservatives actively persist in forging a link between property and citizenship, and secondly, because of the view that a community bound by property rights is the type of community that they are seeking to maintain, be it because of natural desires, historical references or financial incentives. Property rights, then serve the purposes of the Modern Conservatives and have thus become an ideological imperative. As such they are able to justify future action. This is not merely due to the property relations themselves, but because of what they help to achieve within a community. Thus I shall shortly explore what it is that property relations serve to do.

However, before doing so I need to raise the issue of tradition. In the discussion of Scruton's definition of conservatism I noted that he believed that it arose:

> ... directly from the sense that one belongs to some continuing and pre-existing social order, and this fact is all important in determining what to do. (1980, p.21)

Scruton is suggesting that conservatism is about the preservation of tradition. The possession of property is the bedrock of this preservation. Thus traditions are maintained by property ownership.

Scruton therefore links Modern Conservatism explicitly with tradition. The particular problem with this conception of tradition is that it is rooted in individual possession. Traditions are preserved because of our individual holdings which give our lives meaning and allow us to exercise our will. But if this is the case how are traditions passed on across generations? Ownership is concerned with excluding others from the benefits of the particular good, whilst traditions are concerned with the sharing of meaning and values. These two processes appear to run counter to each other. The privatism of ownership is unlikely to inculcate communal values and meanings that become reinforced into traditions.

Indeed I would suggest that a concern with ownership has the effect of destroying tradition by, firstly, emphasising the market as the main mechanism for the provision of goods and services, and secondly, by the imposition of a particular set of values and meanings that override pre-existing forms of social order. Markets are defined as impersonal, innovative and unsentimental processes which operate according to maximising criteria. They are therefore likely to encourage the jettisoning of institutions and forms of behaviour that do not assist in maximising short term economic gains.

Modern Conservatism does not conserve, but rather it seeks to create (of course, it would say recreate) a particular social order that it believes existed before the advent of massive state intervention. It seeks to impose a "tradition" that it feels once existed, and can be restored by a renewed emphasis on property ownership. What this so-called tradition consists of and why it is considered worth recreating is to be examined next.

2.5 Property and The Significance of Housing

I began the last section by stressing the distinction between the Modern Conservative notion of citizenship and that of social democracy. The social democratic view was to guarantee citizens their political, social and civil rights to ensure that they are fully able to participate in the community. Individuals are defined by their relationship with the community. In effect the community has developed a bundle of apparently necessary rights which all citizens have. All citizens are equal within the community, with no one having more or less (even when an individual would voluntarily give up or transfer these rights to another). The social democratic view was thus fundamentally a permissive or positive exposition of freedom and rights.

The Modern Conservatives, however, have purported to pursue a negative concept of freedom. They are not particularly concerned to maintain the rights of citizens in relation to the community, but rather to protect the rights one individual citizen has in relation to others. Instead of a concern for equality, the emphasis is on the protection of an individual's right to pursue his or her aims so long as in doing so others are not themselves constrained. Hence freedom is expressed in negative terms, of protecting the individual from constraint (Hayek, 1982). The Modern Conservative does not therefore seek to define the individual in any particular terms, hoping rather to construct laws and structures that allow the individual the freedom to characterise him or herself.

The Modern Conservative view depends upon a Kantian view of freedom. Human beings are capable of acting with will. They are rational beings able to differentiate between concepts and issues, and to undertake considered decision making. This is contrasted with non-human animals who are capable merely of drives and desires. Being more worthy, humans are thus seen as ends in themselves and it is therefore not morally permissible to use them as means to achieve other ends. This applies regardless of the merits of the ends to which the means are to be applied. As such humans may not be sacrificed against their will for the good of the community (see Nozick, 1974, pp. 32-3 for a fuller discussion of this particular issue).

The social democratic ideal presupposes a particular set of social relations in which individual citizens find themselves placed. Modern Conservatives state that this inevitably involves the direction and conscription of individual citizens to meet these aims. In particular the ideas of social justice and income distribution are picked out as indicative of the state using citizens as means rather than ends in themselves. (Green, 1987; Hayek, 1990; Shand, 1982). Humans are therefore seen as autonomous agents who may not be used to meet the aims of the collective. Modern Conservatives see rights as protecting individuals. They do not necessarily give them anything, other than the not inconsiderable ability to pursue their own ends free from constraint.

Thus the right to property can be seen as the freedom of individuals to use what they own as they see fit, provided it does not constrain the property rights of others. A concern for private property is therefore a concern with the individual and their empowerment. Individuals should be given the opportunity, by laws protecting property, to pursue their independence.

This idea of the individual capable of independent action is at the centre of the Modern Conservative view of the social order, and it is what property rights seek to allow, develop and protect. With these rights in place two essential elements of the social order will develop. Firstly, property rights allow for a free market where individuals voluntarily exchange their property. Secondly, ownership of property allows the independent agent to take personal moral responsibility for his or her actions. Both these facets promote a self-interested and introspective view of the world aimed at re-establishing and maintaining a particular set of values.

This belief in freedom and independence is mirrored in the terminology of the 1987 White Paper and it is worth returning to the key sections of this document. The government states that "home ownership gives people independence" (DOE, 1987, p.2) This is followed with the contention that ownership "gives (the owners) a sense of greater personal responsibility" (p. 2).

Independence and responsibility are thus linked through home ownership. This passage goes on to state that independence and greater personal responsibility "are important factors in the creation of a more stable and prosperous society" (p.2). It follows therefore that that which encourages and supports independence and personal responsibility is worthy of government support and subsidy. A stable social order is thus enhanced by home ownership, because of the increase in the amount of these two facets it brings about.

The Modern Conservatives, of course, are not merely interested in the issues of independence and responsibility as abstract ideals. They have not, and do not, act without some particular purpose in mind. They are intent on implementing a particular set of policies leading to a desired set of outcomes (whether they are achieved or even likely to be is not especially relevant at this point). It is therefore not enough to merely discuss independence per se, but rather what it is that the individual home owner has independence from and to do. What constraints, obligations, or ties are individual households, by becoming home owners, freeing themselves from? In addition, once free, what are they then able to do? These two questions are, of course, linked, and I shall attempt to answer them together.

Regarding the issue of who or what one is freed from we can again turn to the 1987 White Paper. The Modern Conservatives believe that the individual needs freeing from the effect and influence of the public sector — from government (but presumably not this government) taking decisions for its citizens. In effect the problem is the social democratic conception of defining the citizen in terms of the community and what the community does for the individual. The White Paper relates this specifically to housing:

> In the public sector too little attention has been paid to the wishes of tenants or to their views on how their requirements can best be met; tenants have generally not been allowed to express their choices

clearly and have therefore not always found the kind of accommodation they want. (DOE, 1987; p.1)

The public sector restricts individuals in their aims and does not allow them to be independent. This is a claim consistently made by conservative thinkers and writers for as long as the state has engineered mass public provision.

Boyson believes that the Welfare State has trapped council tenants. The taxation to pay for council housing has impoverished them and made it harder for them to purchase their own home. In addition the system of allocation by bureaucratic rationing serves to create labour immobility and fuels unemployment. Good quality housing is so rare, and its allocation so arbitrary, that once a tenant has found a suitable property he or she will stay there. Such a situation is allowed because of income maintenance and welfare services provided by the state. These views of the effects of welfare on unemployment and labour mobility are also discussed by Albon and Stafford (1987) and Minford, Peel and Ashton (1987).

A more general picture is given by Green (1987) who tries to draw some conclusions about the Modern Conservative view of state welfare provision:

> The common theme is that individuals should be able to direct their own lives to a far greater extent than is now possible, and that one of the chief obstacles to greater self-direction is the over-mighty state. (p. 210)

The problem caused by the state, particularly with regard to local authority housing, is that it ignores supply and demand:

> Divorced from real measures of demand, councils have built many hundreds of thousands of houses and flats which are now difficult to let. (p. 185)

The mode of local authority provision is such that tenants — the customers — are unable to exercise any effective preference with regard to the product which they receive. They must take what is offered them by a monolithic, unresponsive supplier, and they have no mechanism for passing on information of their dissatisfaction to the supplier.

Tenants are denuded of their independence because there is no market in which they may exercise their individual choice.

The social democratic view of government, which favoured public intervention and provision, concerned itself with inclusive and generally applicable forms of citizenship. The emphasis was thus on distribution, or rather redistribution of income. Social democracy did not then regard private property with absolute sanctity. The Modern Conservatives, however, are distinguished by their opposition to social and civil rights and in their stead place a support for economic freedom. Political rights are seen as derivative of the nature of support given to economic rights. It these latter rights that allow us to participate in society and empower us. Social democrats would rather see political rights as derivative of the social.

Economic freedom is intimately linked with rights to property. Property rights can be defined as the freedom to use our property as we would wish, subject to necessary constraints protecting the property of others. However, property rights also entail the ability to voluntarily transfer and exchange our property. We have the right to sell, to trade, or indeed to give it away. Additionally we have the right to exclude others from the use of our property (as far as it is possible to avoid externalities and the difficulties in extracting compensation from third parties). Finally, we have the right to not use our property and if we so desire to destroy it. Of course, in practice these rights are hedged around with legislative and moral constraints concerning taxation, planning restrictions, heritage, pollution and environmental issues, etc. This is without considering the effect that the use of our property may have on the ability of another to function and freely use what is ours. As Nozick (1974) states, he may leave his knife where he pleases, but not in another's chest. Thus our property rights are not absolute (and this, of course, creates major problems for Nozick's thesis on the minimal state). But we can still describe the general attributes of use (in the widest sense that includes total inactivity), transferability and excludability.

The significance of these factors is that they allow a market to operate. That we have an exclusive right to use a good gives it a particular value. This is determined both by what it is used for, and also by the possibility of excluding others from its use. It is thus a private good. Excludability from the use of property means that those so excluded must pursue alternative means in order to obtain its use. This may involve force, theft or deception, but these methods are unstable and unpredictable because of laws and supporting agencies designed to protect against illicit appropriation. Thus, if those seeking the use of a good are not prepared to risk legal sanction, they must persuade the current owner to voluntarily transfer or extend the right of use to them. Such a transfer may be in the form of an exchange for something which the current owner finds more desirable; as a gift; or, more commonly, by the payment of compensation. A system of compensated voluntary transfer is a market. A market therefore is where individuals seeking to fulfil their desires come together to exchange and transfer their property to their assumed mutual advantage. Thus without exclusive ownership a market could not exist.

A free market is then essential to all forms of conservatism that relies on property rights for its legitimisation. Whilst writers such as Scruton (1980) assert that conservatism is not necessarily capitalist, a free market is an inevitable consequence of the reliance of property rights and the emphasis on the individual freedom to exercise these rights as the individual sees fit. Therefore flowing out of the right to property is economic freedom within a market.

Levitas (1986) has stated that there are three themes that define the Modern Conservative social order. Firstly, there is a concentration on accountability. However, this is not accountability to the electorate or to citizens in general, but to the consumer. Consumer sovereignty is to be extended as the supreme arbiter. This theme is echoed by Clarke, Cochrane and Smart (1987) who see the reciprocity between rights and obligations that characterised the Beveridge era being ignored by the Modern Conservative governments. Instead they have focused on the role of the citizen as a consumer, and as a taxpayer — as those who pay for government services. This issue of the citizen as taxpayer is important in Modern Conservative thinking. We are taxed on our property and on our ability to obtain property (i.e., our income). The state is thus appropriating a portion of our property to carry out its policies. Whether this appropriation is seen as forced or voluntarily sanctioned depends upon the particular citizen's view of the state and the particular policies being pursued. The level of taxation levied, however, inevitably affects the ability of the consumer to exercise his/her choices in the market.

Secondly, Levitas identifies the issue of efficiency, which is determined on the basis of meeting effective demand rather than dealing with problems that affect society as a whole and detract from its cohesiveness. It is a concern with meeting economic welfare according to Pareto optimality criteria, rather than on social welfare grounds as defined by Beveridge's attempt to defeat the five giant evils.

Thirdly, Levitas states that the Modern Conservatives are concerned with freedom, defined as the absence of restraint. Modern Conservative freedom is that of individual action, free from state involvement and thus the emphasis is on the deregulation and the limitation of the state.

These three characteristics, which Levitas rightly sees as central, are all defined in economic terms and relate back to the citizen's rights to property ownership.

Levitas' discussion can be extended by suggesting that the characteristics of accountability and efficiency rely on economic freedom. Accountability implies a degree of independence and the ability to act freely on the part of the holder of that right. Another individual or agency, in this case the state, is being restrained and restricted in order to enhance the rights of the property holder as a taxpayer. Efficiency is here defined in terms of allowing the individual the ability to express their voluntary preferences, or rather to exercise their right to use, exchange and transfer property rights to achieve their optimum and therefore economically efficient level of satisfaction. Accountability and efficiency therefore allow the individual economic agent the freedom from the restraints imposed by an overmighty state and the demands of others. The individual is thus able to pursue his or her own private aims. It is a view that sees property as an economic resource to be used as individuals see fit (Ryan, 1987).

Property thus allows us to participate in a market, and the market allows property to become active — to become an asset used to pursue our own self interest. This identification with property as an economic asset is crucial to an understanding of Modern Conservatism and its political success after 1979. It is now possible to relate this economic imperative with the second concern of Modern Conservatism, of the need for a heightened sense of moral responsibility.

However, before doing so, it is necessary to dispel the potential objection that I have confused economic liberalism with Modern Conservatism. It has been stated, for instance, that Hayek, whose ideas have been taken as representing the form of market relations described above, is not really a conservative at all (Green, 1987; Shand, 1990). Whilst I would agree that much of Hayek's work would appear to be antithetical to the Modern Conservatives, particularly with regard to his concept of the spontaneous change and development and his rejection of intuitism (Shand, 1990), several of his ideas have been adopted by them. Thus regardless of Hayek's explicit protestations (postscript to Hayek, 1960) and those of his supporters, he is used as a reference point. Indeed we could not fully understand the Modern Conservative programme in government without a knowledge of Hayek.

I can make two points on this issue. Firstly, it is a mistake to see political action as being an example of purity. There is a contradiction between the liberal and conservative strands of what is termed the New Right (and indeed I shall make much of this in the following chapter). But this may be of no particular concern to the politicians involved, (at least for as long as their policies appear to work). They are rather content to use those ideas that appear most convenient and fit in with their overall view. If several of Hayek's ideas help to justify what is often an intuitive world view, then it is not surprising that they will be taken up, almost regardless of the authors intentions. It is not terribly relevant that these ideas may not be entirely representative of Hayek's work, or that certain aspects of conservatism such as the overriding authority of the state and the duty of citizens to the social order, contradict them. There is after all a considerably long history — at least dating back to Plato and his Socratic dialogues — of using the ideas (ostensible or otherwise) of another for one's own purposes. A notable example is that of Marx turning Hegel's idealism on its head. There is thus nothing unusual in the selective use of ideas to develop (dare I say dialectically?)

a new ideology. Nor should it imply cynicism on the part of the usurper, for where else are they expected to get ideas from than the political and intellectual traditions of which they are part? Furthermore, should we really always expect the perfect assimilation of these ideas, and not that they be filtered through the prejudices and interpretations of the recipients?

Secondly, as I have discussed earlier, we should distinguish between the Modern Conservatives, with a political programme forged in the realities of political power, and the concept "conservatism". The latter concept, of conservatism, is both a historical and an international one. It could be applied to Disraeli, Salisbury, Baldwin and Heath in all their diversity; of the ideas of Plato, Burke and Oakeshott; and of Reagan in the USA and Kohl in Germany. It is therefore a general position that favours and attempts to preserve traditions and looks to the past (amongst other things). There is thus both conservatism in general and specific conservatisms.

However, the past is always being added to and thus traditions develop. Modern Conservatism is derived from the conservative tradition, but it does not necessarily typify it. This untypicality (which, as it were, is not unique) is largely because the Modern Conservatives have incorporated several of the ideas of liberals such as Hayek and libertarians such as Nozick. Whether these thinkers would wish their ideas to be so used is not relevant to the majority of politicians (nor indeed to the current writer!). Nor do the politicians necessarily seek the endorsement of thinkers for their wider aims. This, of course, does not stop the followers of Hayek claiming the credit on his behalf for the intellectual change in political culture across the world on his behalf (see Kresge and Wenar's introduction to Hayek, 1994).

I have shown that the Modern Conservatives see a link between economic freedom and property via a market for private goods. Such a freedom allows for a more accountable and efficient allocation of resources. But the Modern Conservatives, whilst making extensive use of economic liberalism to justify property rights, do not attempt to rely on it exclusively. Their ideological construction of private property rights has other props than just the economic.

Ownership of property and activity within an unregulated market is seen to derive a moral benefit. It is said to actually improve us ethically. This relates to the rather intuitive regard for property noted in the work of Scruton (1980). This moral justification for a free market, and thus for property, is discussed by Marquand (1988):

> It is only in the free, competitive market that men and women can realise themselves and their aspirations without interference from others. (p. 163)

In such a market consumers:

> ... are themselves, acting for themselves, choosing themselves, and responsible for their own actions ... (p. 163)

Whilst Marquand is largely critical of this concept, he has identified two of the key notions attached to property rights. He talks of consumers "choosing themselves" and of their being "responsible for their own actions". The ownership of private property, which gives us access to markets, allows us to express a choice and to take responsibility. I have shown that these notions have been deployed by the Modern Conservatives in the 1987 White Paper. Further I have shown how they have criticised the public sector for its lack of these attributes. A state which provides for the welfare needs of its citizens is seen as being morally disabling. It merely creates a dependency culture where individuals become incapable of independent decision making. Centrally provided welfare turns citizens into "wards of the state" (Friedman, quoted in Green, 1987, p.80).

The theme that state provision creates a dependent citizenry is a common one amongst conservative thinkers and politicians. A typical exposition is given by Boyson (1978). The problem derives from the inability of citizens to see the linkage between what they pay in taxation and what they receive back in the benefits from the state. The process does not involve a direct transaction, as would occur in a free market, but rather involves extraction by one agency and the provision of services by others, both of which are outside the direct control of the individuals themselves. This divorce of payment from the receipt of services leads to excess supply, which is irresponsible:

If any service is 'free' people will ask for more, for speedier service, for higher quality service, without needing to count the cost. (Boyson, 1978; p.96)

As payment is not made directly the service is seen as free and thus, without price as a rationing mechanism, demand is unlimited. Such a situation, according to Boyson, is morally wrong as it stifles individual effort and responsibility: it hampers the "moral growth" (p.110) of the individual. Nor is this, in Boyson's view, merely a case of misplaced good intentions:

A state that does for its citizens what they can do for themselves is an evil state; and a state which removes all choice and responsibility for its people and makes them like broiler hens will create the irresponsible society. (quoted in Clarke, Cochrane and Smart, 1987; p.133)

Boyson is here backed by Seldon who contends that "(h)elping people weakens the will to self help" (quoted in Clarke, Cochrane and Smart, 1987, p. 138). Offering support and assistance to people is thus seen as counterproductive. It disables them, and also by implication, merely perpetuates the need for support and assistance. It is thus stated that if help is given to alleviate particular circumstances, the numbers experiencing those circumstances appears to increase (the Housing (Homeless Persons) Act 1977 is often given as an example of this "phenomenon").

Several interesting points may be pulled out of this discussion. Firstly, we should note that whilst human beings are generally seen as being capable, this capability must be constantly reinforced. If humans are not conditioned into the correct moral behaviour they will quickly fall into irresponsibility. It is a view that emphasises the "fallen" nature of humankind, whereby a return to a barbaric state of nature is a constant possibility, held off by the merest veneer of civilisation.

The second point flows out of this. If humans are quick to descend into irresponsibility what may prevent it? The Modern Conservatives believe that it is the state which protects the citizenry from themselves. Scruton (1980) draws an analogy of the family with authority in the state. Government is seen as the parent and the citizen as the child. The child is what he or she is by virtue of the parent and therefore the parent has an obligation to form and influence the child's development. The obligation of the child is built not on a call to justice, but rather on respect, honour and piety. Scruton sees the role of the state as forming and developing the citizen and protecting them in return for the due respect and supplication. Therefore the citizen, according to Scruton, has no identity without, or outside of the state.

What this implies is that the citizens have to be pushed and directed into taking responsibility and exercising choice. This, of course, means that the state has decided what is a responsible act, and is thus able to determine what choices are allowable and morally correct. It is an approach that is essentially authoritarian and centralising, aimed at achieving greater independence on the part of the individual citizens (this rather obvious contradiction will be ignored at present, but it is an issue which I shall return to in the following chapter).

This authoritarian view helps to provide a further link between property and moral responsibility. A privatised form of provision aimed at heightening responsibility serves to re-emphasise the role of the family as the basic social unit within a society. It is our family members for whom and to whom we are responsible, and with whom we exercise choice. Clarke, Cochrane and Smart (1987) state that privatisation has involved the attempt to remoralise the family. Privatisation, where families are responsible for their own welfare will, it is suggested, leads to a revival of the traditional virtues of family life. These virtues are seen to need re-emphasis in the face of increasing levels of lone parenthood, divorce, crime, child abuse, drug abuse and so on. Additionally the Modern Conservatives see the family as a bulwark against sexual permissiveness, multiculturalism and liberal social values (Levitas, 1986b; Loney, 1987). The Modern Conservative view of the family is essentially of a heterosexual, paternalistic and introverted unit resistant to change.

Furthermore, the family is where many of the caring and philanthropic activities within the community ought to take place. It is the family which should provide for the needs of its members, and in doing so the family members are able to exercise choice, take on responsibility and thus grow as moral beings.

The Modern Conservatives thus stress the significance of the home as a place where the primary social relations should, and do, take place. In order for this to occur properly the family needs to be able to assert its rights against intrusion and to ensure its own security (Scruton, 1980; Saunders, 1990). It is only by being able to exclude others that we are fully able to operate as an independent family unit. We cannot assert ourselves as responsible agents if intrusion is allowed into the home. Thus choice and responsibility are made possible through rights to private property which emphasise excludability and freedom from intrusion.

I have therefore shown the reasons why private property is so significant for the Modern Conservatives. Firstly, it allows citizens to be active in a market and thus to exercise individual freedom. Secondly, it allows for the remoralisation of individuals, enhancing their self-reliance. Thus property is said to offer freedom and independent individual action. In the next chapter these themes will be addressed to develop a critique of Modern Conservatism and its attendant housing policy.

CHAPTER THREE

THE FAILURE OF MODERNIST HOUSING POLICY

3.1. The Contradictions of Modern Conservatism

My discussion up to now has been seeking to identify the main ideological themes that run through Modern Conservative housing policy, and to show why it is that there has been such a concentration on provision and the consequent commodification of housing. I have stated that this emphasis on provision is not particular to the Modern Conservatives and that commodification is not a phenomenon unique to them (Forrest and Murie, 1988; Malpass and Murie, 1990). Post war social democratic governments, with their rather different emphasis on production, distribution and on the need for intervention in markets, still concentrated on the provision of housing as the basis of policy. However, although these policies may have led to a certain amount of commodification (and assisted in perpetuating it), this could be said to be because of their failure to fully understand the interrelationship of housing and economic policy. The Modern Conservatives, however, as Levitas (1986) has shown, have emphasised the economic to the relative exclusion of the other forms of public behaviour. I have also shown that the other aspects of their rhetoric, particularly regarding freedom and responsibility, stem out of this economic imperative.

Thus instead of a policy aimed at the use of housing based on the significance of human dwelling, it is concerned solely with housing as property. Housing is seen as a private good and it can therefore be said to be monetised, in that it is defined by its exchange value. Therefore the significant issue relating to housing in the 1990s is its organisation in a market. It is seen as one of the principal variables on which the national economy depends. Indeed this concentration is frequently seen by economists such as Muellbauer (1990) and Ermish (1990) as one of, if not the major cause of Britain's economic difficulties in the 1980s and 1990s. This is because of the linkage between house purchase, borrowing and debt, and in turn with interest rates and the financial markets generally.

As a result we have a situation where policy is developing and maintaining housing provision through a market. Housing has become commodified and the nature of housing is merely one more private good traded in the market by self-interested consumers. Our homes — the place where we dwell — have become inextricably linked with the national economy as the recession in the housing market in the early 1990s has shown.

I wish to make two further points about the operation of markets. Firstly, we cannot conceive of a market that is not influenced by the past. A market cannot be created *ex nihilo*, but rather we can only aim to develop, moderate and influence existing conditions. In addition, we must accept that certain players in a market will succeed, whilst others will fail. Therefore the players in a market do not necessarily retain their positions, either absolutely or relative to each other. It is inevitable that certain players will already have gained, or will be able to gain control ever more resources and thus gain power in the market. This restricts the ability of others to achieve their desires and aims. In practice many consumers face only a limited choice and may therefore find it difficult to obtain appropriate housing. This situation is indeed particularly prevalent in a housing market. Supply is inelastic because of limitations on productivity, factor immobility and scarcity. Furthermore consumers have imperfect knowledge because of price differentials and infrequency of purchase (Legrand and Robinson, 1984). Allied to this is the oligopolistic nature of the financial sector which further hampers the ability of consumers to make free choices.

The second issue is that once a market is established the individual citizen has no option but to participate. The possibilities for fulfilling our needs are limited if we are not prepared to play in the market. Thus we are given no choice but to take on the responsibility imposed by the market. However, if we are forced into a choice, what form of freedom is it? We would expect freedom of action to include the possibility of taking no action — the status quo must always be an option.

I mentioned in the previous chapter that the Modern Conservatives have a specific vision of what moral responsibility means. It is where the family is seen as the basic social unit with its members caring for each other and exhibiting an apparently intuitive altruism. It is the security given by the relationship within the home that allows for the stable operation of a free market. However, there is a major contradiction evident in the attempted linkage of the market and the family in the home. As Jordan (1989) has pointed out we act in the home in a manner that is the very opposite of how we are supposed to have acted to obtain it in the first place:

> Within the bosom of the family, self-interested producers and con-sumers are transformed into self-sacrificing, caring, sharing partners, parents and relatives, and individual striving is set aside in favour of the pursuit of other's good. (p. 144)

We act in a self-interested manner in the market in order to maximise our utility or profit, and then we return to the home and apparently negate this very image out of love for our family. Within the home we are seen as being prepared to make any sacrifice and undertake any hardship. Clearly there is a problem with a belief that states we can ob-tain a particular condition through self-interest, yet only maintain it by self-sacrifice.

This is merely one example of the contradiction that lies at the heart of Modern Conservatism. The cause of this is its rather eclectic ideological development that has sought to fuse the economic liberalism and individualism of Hayek (1982), with the traditional, hierarchical and intuitive brand of conservatism typified by Scruton (1980). The result is a government that has consistently centralised power and resources in the name of choice, freedom and responsibility. This creates the paradox of the government wielding its power in order to lessen the power of government.

There has been a considerable body of work concerned with these contradictions, either seeking to highlight or mitigate them (for ex-ample, see Levitas, 1986; Loney, 1987; Gamble, 1988; Green, 1988; Shand, 1990; and Skidelsky, 1988). What is important with this con-tradiction is not whether Modern Conservatism is logically inconsistent, as we would expect a degree of eclecticism from most political ideologies, but rather what are its implications for political practice from attempting to weld together two such contradictory notions about the nature and role of the state. My concern with Modern Conservatism is as a working ideology which has helped to create a programme of policy. The interest is in the attempt to unravel what has happened as a result of its operation and why the aims of policy may not have been met.

The negation of Modern Conservatism as a viable political project derives from the practical effects on the individual from the two sides of the ideology justifying property rights. Economic liberalism places the individual at the centre of its intellectual framework. Hayek's methodological individualism describes individuals as the constituents of the social order. The community is merely the sum of its parts and no more (Shand, 1990). Yet Scruton's description (1980) of a transcendent, intuitive conservatism portrays the state as the absolutist parent and the citizen as the dependent child. These views are incompatible and lead to the individual being forced into a particular set of imperatives that have been characterised by the term "the property owning democracy". Thus, from the starting point of a negative definition of freedom that seeks only to protect individuals from coercion, the Modern Conservatives have developed a housing policy that positively prescribes what is most beneficial for the individual.

However, if the ideology of Modern Conservatism is contradictory, how can the position be maintained? The answer lies in the fact that Hayek's individualism has a purely economic definition. His economic freedom is concerned only with the individual's role in the market and it is thus consistent with a moral perspective based on self reliance and responsibility. Indeed we can only be free, according to Hayek, in a market system. All other possible systems deny the individual this freedom. We are given no choice by Hayek in this matter. The state, so minded, effectively forces the citizen into this role, as a parent directs and circumscribes the behaviour of a child.

This de facto enforcement arises because of the apparently spontaneous nature of a market order (Hayek, 1982). Hayek suggests that a market system has developed not by design, but rather from the combined effects of millions of individual actions. It is spontaneous in the sense that there has been no attempt to design or create a particular social order. Hayek is thus suggesting that the market order, favoured by the Modern Conservatives, is an example of the non-patterned principle identified by Nozick (1974) as an important element for a liberal description of social life.

However, Nozick himself is able to show that Hayek's form of economic liberalism is itself a patterned principle of distribution, even though Hayek has strongly suggested that such a pattern will lead to an erosion of freedom. According to Nozick, Hayek's thesis calls for a distribution based on the perceived benefits we have given to others. Nozick describes Hayek's principle as:

> To each according to how much he benefits others who have the resources for benefiting those who benefit them. (1974, p.158)

Thus Nozick criticises economic liberalism for contradicting its essential nature. It is the imposition of a particular pattern of distribution which therefore actually delimits freedom by offering one particular solution and no alternative. This implies, and I shall show that this is the case in the next section, that the maintenance of Hayek's spontaneous order necessitates the active intervention of government, regardless of whether it arose spontaneously or not.

Modern Conservatism, whilst subscribing to the Kantian view of freedom, actually denies it. This is because it attempts to prescribe and proscribe types of behaviour in order to achieve a particular social order. Scruton, despite his avowed Kantianism (1984), presents the preservation of the authority of the state above the rights of citizens (1980). Citizens are seen as the means of achieving the ends of the Modern Conservative social order. Modern Conservatism does not therefore bear out its promise of furthering the role of the individual. This is precisely because it tries to imbue the citizen with a general purpose.

Contrary to the ideology of the Modern Conservatives, we do not have a homogeneous moral purpose, and our behaviour is not predictive on the basis of a generalised ideology. The particular error has been to portray human beings as primarily economic agents motivated by self-interest. In practice, of course, we are considerably more complex than the concept of economic freedom would allow. We do not necessarily place any greater moral virtue on market activities than others such as leisure, social intercourse and the family. We are motivated by other things besides profit, utility and income. Indeed the description of property as an economic asset is at odds with much of our daily lives. Property ownership does not characterise us or determine our lives, but it rather allows us to undertake a range of activities. In fact it may even allow us to escape from the market itself. As Rose (1989) has stated:

> Instead of considering a house as an investment asset, most people think of a house as a home and a centre of non-market activities. (p. 139)

In addition the purported relationship between property and morality breaks down. Jordan (1987) states that in reality we do not identify private property and the market with justice:

> In real life no one acts as if private property, capitalist industry or the market have anything to do with fairness. They are simply treated as efficient and convenient ways of optimising the use of resources and price opportunities under certain circumstances. All of us — rich and poor — use markets when they suit our purposes, but we spend much of our lives protecting ourselves from their adverse consequences. The rich accumulate privileges and property holdings for themselves and their families; the poor try to preserve informal resources and networks so that they have something to fall back on adversity. Far from accepting market conditions or outcomes as fair, we act as if their only justice lies in their allowing us to hedge against them in various ways without withdrawing from them altogether. (p. 58)

Markets are used when they suit our purposes as defined by ourselves, not the imperatives of government.

Rose (1989) also believes that people are much more pragmatic in their relation to a market:

> In terms of total welfare in the family, a money income remains a sum of money, whatever the source. A house is a roof over one's

head, whoever maintains it, and a meal can have the same amount of calories, whether prepared at home or bought in a restaurant. (p. 146)

Put into other words, ends matter more than the means of achieving them, and to most people the market is just one means amongst several others.

The issue is not then about the "correctness" or otherwise of the ideology, as this is a normative question, but the effects of the generalisation and imposition of a particular set of values. An ideology can be neither correct nor incorrect. What is important is what happens when policies determined by an ideology are implemented. The problem with Modern Conservatism is that it is contradictory and therefore fails to succeed in its aims to control housing policy. The result is that policy determined by such an ideology is unsustainable.

3.2. The Unsustainability of Modern Conservatism

I have suggested that the housing policy of Modern Conservatism has been motivated by ideology and that an understanding of this ideology should precede any analysis of the context within which policy making takes place. Furthermore, I have suggested that policy making was seen to be constructed in a modernist framework, where technical problems are identified and solutions applied by experts. Thus the ideology dictates the possibilities and these are rigidly applied as absolute definitive answers to complex problems.

The particular ideology of Modern Conservatism is one of economic individualism and personal responsibility. The proposed solution is thus one of privatisation and individual ownership. It was believed that a shift from collective to individual provision would improve quality and choice in housing.

In pursuing this policy the Modern Conservative government had to maintain a certain level of public provision for those unable to fulfil their needs through owner occupation. The legislation in 1988 and 1989 recognised this, but attempted to shift the balance of provision to housing associations and to increase these organisations' reliance on private financing. It aimed to increase the private sector's involvement in public provision and went to the extent of redefining housing associations as part of the so called, "independent rented sector" (DOE, 1987).

The result of this policy has been to link housing provision — both private and public — more firmly into the economy. The majority of households purchase properties within a market using finance obtained from competing private sector financial institutions. The remainder are increasingly to be housed by housing associations who must attract private finance in the face of competing investment opportunities.

The state of the economy is an increasingly important factor for housing association procurement and development, more so now that the government does not cushion public sector provision from direct contact with the economy through the relatively open-ended deficit subsidies enjoyed between 1974 and 1989. Thus the long term stability of interest rates is now as important to housing associations as it is to those with mortgages.

However, the relationship between housing provision and the economy is more complex than a mere link between economic activity and the number of dwellings provided. The housing market is seen as being a major determinant of economic activity itself. Eatwell (1992) states that the housing market was largely responsible for the consumer boom of the late 1980s. The subsidisation of the market through tax relief and the deregulation of housing finance led to a house price spiral that in turn "encouraged and sustained the boom in consumer borrowing" (Eatwell, 1992, p. 22). Owner occupiers were gaining access to the increased equity in their housing and using this for both housing and non-housing expenditure. Hutton (1992) states that equity withdrawal doubled between 1983 to 1988 and "in 1988 homeowners took as much as 26bn out of the equity of their homes" (Hutton, 1992, p. 61). The potential for equity withdrawal was indeed considerable with housing capital valued at 1000bn and outstanding mortgage debt of only 300bn (Housing Review, Vol. 41; no. 2).

Equity withdrawal served to fuel a consumer boom that in turn increased demand for housing and therefore its price. This allowed equity withdrawal to be maintained as it was a function of rising house values relative to historic mortgage debt. The willingness of households to withdraw equity from their housing, and thus to incur additional debt, was dependent on expectations of both future house price increases and of the prospects for the economy as a whole.

The problem with this situation, of course, was that a consumer boom built upon debt and appreciating nominal house values was not sustainable. In 1990 the government was forced to respond to rapidly increasing inflation and it did so by increasing interest rates and thus the housing costs of those with mortgages. The government, through this policy of targeting, appeared to be in no doubt as to the cause of the economy's overheating. The result, as intended was a capping of demand and house price rises. However, the non-intended outcome was a general recession and a considerable realignment of the relationship between house price values and housing debt.

Indeed, the extent of the fall in house prices was such that in November 1992 1.4 million house buyers, or one in seven, were suffering from negative equity, where the value of their property was less than the outstanding mortgage debt (Hughes, 1992). The majority of those suffering from this problem had bought property since 1987. The persistence of this situation is likely to have a major, and potentially long term, dampening effect on economic activity as it effectively traps households in their property unless they are prepared to take a considerable loss on its sale. But as negative equity is due to a depressed market it is not necessarily the case that these houses could be sold.

This situation raises an issue often overlooked when domestic property is seen solely as an asset. We may sell our property and realise an amount of capital, but we will almost certainly have to use this to replace the dwelling we have sold (as I shall demonstrate in Chapter Five, housing need is a permanent condition). It is also obvious that if the value of the property we have sold has appreciated, then so will the value of others, probably including the one we are seeking to buy. Therefore our "wealth" may only be illusory, in the sense it is not effectively realisable, except in periods of rapid house price inflation. Even in this latter case it is only partially so, depending on the difference between the outstanding debt on the property and its current value.

The recession caused a further problem for many households, that of affordability. Whilst house prices had fallen, the effect of interest rate increases was to increase housing costs. Therefore at a time of increasing unemployment there was a considerable increase in the level of mortgage arrears. Cole (1992) states that mortgage repossessions due to arrears rose from 16,000 in 1989 to 76,000 in 1991, and the numbers in arrears for 6 months or more rose from 81,000 to 275,000 (1992, p.85).

Thus house prices fell at a time of increasing housing costs. This was in response to government action and is consistent with the link between housing and the economy. The problem for the government, however, was that it could not control the contraction of the housing market once it had begun. The policy did not have a purely technical effect on one part of the economy that could be contained by specific measures. This is because the relation between housing and the economy is not a directly causal one. In particular the effect of, and on, expectations could not be forecast. For instance, if households expect house prices to fall, and furthermore feel insecure about their long term employment prospects, they will not increase their consumption in response to government exhortation or to changes in policy that leave their indebtedness untouched. As Eatwell has stated with regard to expectations, "(i)t only needs everyone to believe houses are worth 10 percent less for them to be actually worth 10 percent less" (1992, p. 22). There is thus a resistance to economic policy that falls outside of the technical competence of policy makers to correct. The government found that the housing market would not readily re-ignite despite a reduction in housing costs as interest rates fell throughout 1992.

However, it still believed that such a re-ignition was necessary as a precursor for economic recovery. It also recognised the political importance of housing, both in terms of the fact that its own political fortunes may rest on the "feel good" factor that appreciating house values bring, and because of the linkage between owner occupation and its rhetoric of individual responsibility in a property owning democracy which, of course, had helped to create the association between a bouyant domestic property market and the Modern

Conservative government's policies. Thus a housing market in long term decline would seriously damage the political project of the Modern Conservatives.

As a result the Modern Conservative government intervened into the market in an attempt to halt the decline, and to encourage households back into the market. Their first initiative was in December 1991 when it persuaded mortgage lenders to make available 1bn for funding so called "mortgage-to-rent" schemes for owner occupiers under threat of repossession. In return the government arranged for income support payments for mortgage interest to be paid directly to lenders rather than to claimants, and to suspend Stamp Duty on the purchase of properties below £250,000 for the period 19 December 1991 to 19 August 1992 (Coles, 1992).

The purpose of this initiative was to reduce the number of mortgage repossessions by 40,000 in 1992, and to act as an incentive for new purchasers. However, the effects were somewhat more limited. Mortgage rescue schemes, either provided directly, or through partnerships with housing associations (who were not party to the negotiations between the government and the mortgage lenders), proved to be complex to arrange. Housing associations were concerned to ensure rents were affordable, and were thus only willing to borrow to purchase potential repossessions at low rates of interest. This however, created difficulties for the lenders who were charging their existing customers not in arrears a higher rate, and who additionally felt they had to protect the money of their investors (Dwelly, 1992). As a result of these problems a mere twelve households had been helped by these schemes by July 1992 (Spittles, 1992).

Indeed the problems surrounding these schemes proved to be insurmountable (Dwelly, 1992) and the most effective response to mortgage arrears was in the form of action taken by the lenders themselves in terms of counselling and rescheduling arrears (Coles, 1992). The significance of this action however was that the Modern Conservatives saw the political necessity in responding to a crisis on home ownership occurring within six months of a General Election. The intervention could be seen therefore as a means of shoring up electoral support by creating a climate in which those in danger of repossession could be "rescued", and thus feel secure with their dwelling. Perhaps of more importance, however, was the impression it gave owner occupiers not in arrears that the tenure was being protected by government action. In this sense the mortgage rescue initiative may have served its purpose in that the Modern Conservatives were re-elected in April 1992, with housing seemingly not being a central issue in the election.

However, the initiative did not halt the decline in house prices. Indeed following sterling's departure from the Exchange Rate Mechanism in September 1992, confidence in the housing market again appeared on the verge of collapse. Thus the government was forced to act in November 1992 to again try and shore up the market. On this occasion though, because of the seriousness of the situation, it was forced to use public funds directly.

In the 1992 Autumn Statement the government announced what became known as the Housing Market Package. This scheme provided 577m to housing associations to buy up repossessions, empty properties from developers and others on the open market before 31 March 1993, and to let these properties to the priority homeless. The aim of the package was explicitly to reinvigorate the market by buying up over 16,000 properties. The Housing Corporation, which was given responsibility for allocating the funding, was in no doubt as to the packages objectives. The Corporation's Chief Executive, Antony Mayer, was quoted as saying that "(t)he aim of this scheme is to kickstart the depressed housing market". He went on, "we believe the scheme offers a real opportunity to revitalise England's flagging housing market" (Housing Associations Weekly, 27.11.92, p. 3).

The clear intention was to purchase as many properties as quickly as possible. Indeed by March 1993 the sale of 18,255 properties had been approved by the Corporation (H A Weekly, 12.3.93). The consequences of this, however, was that a considerable number of the properties purchased did not necessarily suit the needs of the priority homeless. A high proportion of one bedroomed properties had been purchased and associations in inner London had found difficulty in achieving their target number of purchases because of the cost limits imposed within the scheme (H A Weekly, 12.3.93).

The government's priorities were emphasised by the cost and time limits imposed to ensure the maximum effect as quickly as possible. Thus whilst over 18,000 new tenancies were created there was no particular attempt to match purchases to needs in particular areas. Purchases were concentrated in areas where properties were cheapest and these were not necessarily suitable for families. Again the intervention into the housing market was aimed at serving a political aim of bolstering the form of housing provision that complemented the ideological agenda of the Modern Conservatives. Indeed this became clear when the indicative funding to housing associations for the three years subsequent to 1992/93 was reduced, apparently to compensate for this extra spending (H A Weekly, 20.11.92). Housing associations were thus being explicitly used to intervene into the market to affect the confidence of owner occupiers.

The outcome of the Housing Market Package was somewhat ambiguous. It could be said to have succeeded in the aim of stemming a collapse in the housing market. Yet it did not serve to re-ignite the market which remained static or in slow decline after 1993. The reason for this was that whilst a large number of empty properties were taken off the market it did nothing to alleviate housing debt. The intervention, of itself, did nothing to reduce housing costs or to increase property values. Thus it failed to change the perception of risk that has now been attached to owner occupation.

This again serves to show the complex interlinkage of housing with the economy and the consequent difficulty of effective policy making within this milieu. An active and appreciating housing market is necessary to increase economic activity and thus create employment opportunities. Yet the fear, and indeed the experience of, unemployment limits the prospects for potential purchasers entering the market.

Both the Housing Market Package and the earlier mortgage rescue initiative were seen as necessary because the housing policy of the government was in danger of collapse. The pursuit of the property owning democracy necessitated a buoyant property market where prices rose steadily to allow for the perception of wealth creation. The relation between household and dwelling was thus commodified, with the significance of housing being stated in its monetary value and the status attached to this. However, this relation proved to be unsustainable, and therefore government found itself with no option but to intervene into the market in order to support it. If the market had collapsed their ideological credibility would have been destroyed along with the well-being of a significant proportion of its electoral constituency.

In addition the history of housing policy development since 1979 had left the Modern Conservatives with few other options. In the face of the collapse of their ideological construct, they could not turn directly to local authorities after a decade of rhetoric about their unsuitability as landlords. The private rented sector was in long term decline and not organisable in the manner possible with the housing association movement. Meanwhile the ideology of home ownership had become so pervasive that there was resistance from homeowners to become tenants as part of the mortgage rescue initiative (Coles, 1992; Spittles, 1992). Attitudes towards owner occupation, and consequently renting as a residual sector, had become so ingrained, that despite the effects of a recession, a policy of encouraging renting was simply not tenable. The rhetoric of building and supporting the property owning democracy was so successful that government could only seek to mitigate its failure by further support.

This shows why the policy of the Modern Conservatives has become increasingly unsustainable. There is a built-in rigidity to the policy. The policy can be characterised by its inflexibility and by a lack of contingency to respond to the differing needs of the community and individuals. It represents a mixture of ideology and possiblism that has led to a centralisation of power around the government's role as economic manager. This, of course, is radically at odds with the ideology itself, with its stressing of individualism and personal solutions.

Thus for the Modern Conservatives, the significance of housing is that it allows households access to the economic and moral advantages of the market. This has a political connotation to the extent that owner occupation is so closely tied to the Modern Conservatives' ideological aims. Therefore the political significance of housing is an economic good and as an indication of economic activity and wealth. As a result they are prepared to intervene into the market to maintain this significant role. Indeed this policy has continued as shown in the Housing Corporations spending plans up to 1996 which show a shift in emphasis away from new build towards housing for sale and incentives to buy (Corporation News, December 1993). Since 1994 an increasing proportion of the Housing Corporation's Approved Development Programme (ADP) has been used for low cost owner occupation schemes such as shared ownership and for the so-called "Tenants' Incentive Scheme" which offers housing association tenants a cash payment to purchase a property on the open market. In 1994/95 nearly 25% of the ADP was allocated to these schemes, at a time when the total expenditure of the Housing Corporation had been cut by 21% (H. Corp News, Dec. 1994). This is a trend that the government wishes to see continuing, as evidenced by a White Paper published in June 1995 entitled, *Our Future Homes: Opportunity, Choice and Responsibility* (DOE, 1995). A Purchase Grant Scheme offering discounts of up to £16000 to housing associations tenants with assured tenancies or whose landlord is a charitable body is to be introduced to allow them to purchase the house in which they currently live. The scheme will be voluntary with regard to existing properties, but the government intends to legislate to make it a condition of future grant aid that tenants be given the right to purchase.

The 1995 White Paper appears to show that the Modern Conservatives' perceptions towards owning and renting are unaltered, and moreover, as its title shows, they have become more explicit about the linkage between tenure and choice and responsibility. The cornerstone of their housing policy remains the encouragement of owner occupation. Therefore, as well as housing association tenants being so encouraged, the White Paper promises that there will be no further cuts in mortgage tax relief until the end of the parliament (up to May 1997). The explicit aim of the White Paper is to extend owner occupation by a further 1.5 million dwellings over the decade to 2005 (DOE, 1995). Thus it suggests that the vast majority of new building will be undertaken by the private sector for this market.

However, in a further development of its marketisation policies begun in 1988, the government aim to encourage local authorities to establish local housing companies to manage some or all of their dwellings. These companies would consist of tenant and local business representation, but with only a minority representation from local councillors. Of course, it is debatable as to whether this initiative will be a significant one, bearing in mind the failure of Tenants' Choice. This is dependent upon the level of pressure which the government is able to exert on local authorities. It should be stated that following the financial measures of the Local Government and Housing Act 1989 the government can now exert a much greater level of control than when the Tenants' Choice proposals were introduced (Malpass et al, 1993).

It is still too early to suggest what the effect of these proposals will be. They may or may not be significant in terms of altering the relationships between the various tenures and institutions that support them. However, the White Paper clearly shows that the Modern Conservatives still intend the same ideological imperatives. Like the Housing Market Package in particular, the Modern Conservatives are trapped within the implications of their own rhetoric. Despite an apparent long term depression in the housing market they find themselves with no alternative but to pursue even higher levels of owner occupation. This can only be achieved by an increasingly pervasive control of the major housing institutions and agencies. The 1995 White Paper may be aiming to extend opportunity, choice and responsibility, but it seemingly can only do so by force.

The Modern Conservative description of significance ignores the role that housing plays at the personal level and as part of the process of dwelling. Significance in a sense has been abstracted from the dwelling itself. A house has significance because of the abstract monetary value placed upon it by the market. It is not what we do with the dwelling or what it allows us to fulfil, but rather its opportunity cost that denotes its significance. Such a view is perhaps not so problematic when the monetary values attributed to housing are rising (accepting, of course, that within this perceptual frame there is a tendency to ignore that it is nominal rather than relative values that are increasing). However, when values are falling the dichotomy between the economic and existential significance of housing is seen. Households dwell because of an existential need — they need the dwelling as a means to achieve their particular ends — yet the process of dwelling has been circumscribed by economic imperatives that have trapped them in a gulf between unaffordability and non-tradability. The housing cannot be sold, but it is also not affordable. Thus our attitude towards the property alters because it no longer fits our expectations. However, we still need a dwelling to fulfil our existential needs.

It is by no means clear in what ways the significance of our housing alters when its monetary value changes. Our perception is indeed that it does, yet the house is as intrinsically useful as previously, in that it provides the same level of amenity and physical and, potentially, emotional security. The dwelling may still perform the same purpose. Yet because the concept of home has become de-coupled from housing it is as if we separate the intimate relations from the monetary value of the vessel in which these relations take place. The implication is that a household could undertake these relations in any vessel provided it is affordable. However, when it is no longer affordable these relations do not matter.

The unsustainability of the Modern Conservative housing policy has also demonstrated that control over the dwelling process does not lie with the individual despite the rhetoric of individualism. The significance of dwelling is prescribed to the individual by a nationalised system that forces us into a private relation with a market.

3.3. Housing Policy and Modernity

This detailed discussion of the housing policy of the Modern Conservatives has been an attempt to give an example of the ways in which modernity subverts the notion of value in the dwelling process, and, in so doing creates an unsustainable situation. However, in what ways can the policy of the Modern Conservatives be seen as typical of modernity? Might not what I have described be a peculiarity of Britain over the last twenty years? This might be contended by some commentators who argue that the mere replacement of the Conservative party by the

Labour party is sufficient; that all that is needed is a government that is more committed to public service and a more humane, less market oriented policies. Such an argument rests upon the uniqueness of the policies pursued since 1979.

However, as a close reading of Modern Conservatism has shown, such a sanguine attitude is misplaced. Modern Conservatism is part of a tradition of modernist intervention that can be traced back to 1945. Moreover, it is part of a phenomena that is international and becoming increasingly so, despite (or perhaps resulting in) the growing nationalism of Modern Conservatism (Giddens, 1994). The purpose of this final section of this chapter is to briefly point to these historical and international links.

Forrest and Murie(1988), to reiterate, insist that 1979 was not so much a definitive change in direction in policy, but rather a dramatic increase in the speed of travel. The Labour government in 1976 had begun the reduction in public subsidy to rented housing. Moreover, through the introduction of local authority Housing Investment Programmes in 1977, central government had developed the mechanism whereby local activity could be controlled (Malpass, 1990). Indeed central government, because of the unitary nature of political authority in Britain, has always been able to control the role and activity of local authorities. Thus it is possible to see the policies pursued by the Modern Conservatives after 1979 as, in a sense, following on from the policies of its predecessors. Of course this is not to suggest that there were not significant differences, nor is it to deny the sincerity of the belief of the Modern Conservatives that they were created something new out of the failures of the past. It also does not seek to belittle the genuine sense of outrage on the part of those groups most affected by the policies.

However, I would suggest that the Modern Conservatives were operating in a manner typical of modernity, and that there are thus similarities with its predecessors. I can show this by returning to what I see as one of the principal contradictions at the heart of the Modern Conservative project. Modern Conservatism called for greater personal responsibility and individual agency, but attempted to achieve this aim by government action. Whilst the aim may show a distinction from the social democracy that went before, the method of implementation was the same. Both social democracy (openly) and Modern Conservatism (perversely) made use of the powers of central government to achieve their aims. It is the responsibility of government to manage the economy and seek to maximise the welfare of the citizens and this remains so whether it is a social democratic government concerned with redistribution of public goods or a Modern Conservative government seeking to lighten the burden of the state on individuals and businesses. Should a problem or crisis arise, be it moral, military or whatever, it is the presumed responsibility of the government of the day to attend to it.

The Modern Conservatives, despite their rhetoric, have still used the full powers at their disposal. Moreover, choice is a faculty that may be exercised only on the terms dictated by government. Local authority tenants were given the choice of opting out of local authority control, but opting into local authority control was not permitted. Tenants were given the right to buy, and thus choose their tenure, but the reduction in choice this gave those on local authority waiting lists was not considered. Resources were shifted to support owner occupation, because this was said to enhance individual choice, but again only at the expense of the choices of those unable to afford to buy even with government subsidy. The means of achieving policy therefore show a high degree of similarity between governments over time.

Thus it would be more pertinent to create a distinction around the technical capability or competence of a government to intervene in an economy or with structures of provision. This is a technical question in that it relates to the physical and intellectual capability to determine questions of national significance. It is about the level of competence that we now associate with modern government with its ability to control technologies of power through instrumental rationality (Foucault, 1980, Toulmin, 1990). This distinction is precisely that of the modern with its predecessor; between the capability of the state to formally govern and the ability to maintain informal practices. Modernity is thus portrayed as the ability to control or police the community, and the individuals within it, through the ubiquity of the technologies of power (Foucault, 1988), and this propensity of governmental responsibility can be associated with what, to follow Foucault again, could be referred to as the *historical apriori* that lies behind the *discursive practices* of modernity (Foucault, 1972). It is taken for granted that government is ultimately responsible and legitimately so. The ideology of Modern Conservatism operates within this epistemological framework.

Indeed this contradiction is not unique to Britain. Priemus (1995) describes the privatisation of Dutch social rented housing through the abolition of subsidy to housing corporations. Not only does this show a direct similarity to the British case, albeit a more drastic example, but Priemus clearly shows that this situation is derived out of government action. It is a change in ideological perspective that has created this change in Dutch housing. Priemus also makes the point that government will still be involved in housing provision, in terms of availability, affordability and quality (1995, p. 154). Government will still be responsible in the sense of "ensuring that" rather than "caring for" (p. 154). Thus whilst there is an apparently fundamental change in housing policy towards commercialisation and private provision this can, firstly, only be achieved by government action, and secondly, will still be supervised by government.

On a more general level Boelhower and van der Heijden (1992), in a comparative study of European housing systems, suggest a four stage process of housing policy formation in the post war period. Firstly, they identify a high level of government involvement, particularly to alleviate housing shortages. The second stage involves an emphasis on housing quality, whilst the third stage shows a concern for distribution and targeting specific groups. The fourth stage involves the re-appearance of qualitative and/or quantitative shortages, with a consequent increase in government involvement in some countries. Boelhower and van der Heijden show that these various stages have not coincided, and indeed it could be said that some countries such as Sweden are only just entering the third stage whilst countries such as France, Germany and Britain reached the fourth stage in the late 1980s (p. 273).

There are problems with the methodology used in this comparison, particularly with regard to the accuracy of periodisation which may only be seen *post factum* and the possibility of stages running parallel in different sectors of the housing system. Moreover its concern with taxonomic reduction demonstrates the very preoccupations of modernist discourse that I have been concerned to disabuse.

However, whilst accepting these caveats, Boelhower and van der Heijden clearly show the pervasiveness of government action throughout Europe since the post war period. Indeed their work is supported in this regard by the rather less detailed, yet more historically embedded study by Power (1993) who describes a convergence of housing policy within European states based around the dual issues of continued government failure alongside an unquestioned belief in the continued legitimacy of government action.

This discussion is not to suggest that the issues across Europe directly mirror those in Britain. Indeed, as Oxley (1995) has demonstrated, there are very real difficulties in comparison caused by differences in definition of social housing, the nature of subsidy, the method of calculating public spending and so on. There are thus very real differences between European states. However, this does not effect the general contention that housing policies across Europe are determined centrally and are totalising to the extent that they seek to pursue a particular series of ends to the exclusion of all others. The means and ends will differ both over time and from country to country, but the epistemological framework of governmental competence persists.

The rest of this essay presents an attempt at a description of significance that decouples the housing process from national economic priorities and shifts it towards the personal — to attach human values to the process instead of material ones. Such a change will not come about merely by the reform of the structures of housing provision, but rather from an intellectual and perceptual shift in the designation of the significance of housing. It can come about only through the recognition of personal agency and the genuine limitation of outside interference. In short, I seek an alternative to property rights as the metaphysical focus of the dwelling process.

PART TWO

THE NEED

FOR LIMITS

CHAPTER FOUR

PLURALISM AND ANTI-ESSENTIALISM

The purpose of the discussion in Part One was to describe a modernist approach to housing policy and its consequences. I have shown that the effect of a centralising ideology is to create a situation that is unstable. I have shown that the particular perversity of this situation is that the Modern Conservatives can only seek to mitigate this unsustainability by pursuing the very policy that created it. The practical support and the rhetoric extolling the virtues of owner occupation had been so successful that an alternative policy was not tenable. The Modern Conservatives have thus created the paradox of the necessity of state intervention to ensure individual responsibility and independence.

However, the concern for the individual shown by the Modern Conservatives is a valid one, in that housing is best identified with primarily at the personal level, rather than the communal. It is an existentially significant process which is used privately and not socially (there is an important distinction here between use, on the one hand, and control and ownership on the other). The problem with the Modern Conservatives therefore is not their purported concern for the individual, but rather the effects of this concern. Individuals are described as being predominantly economic agents to the exclusion of the roles of carer, parent, partner and family member. More generally, the problem is that individuals are portrayed as having a specific human nature. The Modern Conservatives seek to describe individuals as having certain common characteristics.

Thus their housing policy has been framed by an ideology that seeks to promote this particular universalised perspective of human nature. This ideology, I have suggested, is typical of modernity. Thus the Modern Conservatives can be differentiated (but not entirely separated) from other more traditional forms of conservative ideology which was framed initially by a reaction to modernity. The Modern Conservatives were shown to be offering an abstract universal vision of human behaviour. It is thus able to define the problems in its own terms — to propose a series of seemingly elemental needs perceived as existentially significant and thus to set an agenda to solve these problems. It is typical of modernity in that there was deemed to be only one possible solution, namely through the market.

Home ownership was seen as natural, and public provision as disabling, with apparently no appreciation of the gradations of use and meaning determined by individual purposes within particular and distinct environments. The effect of this situation is the tendency to see that if the world is at odds with the idealised model, then it is the world that is in need of correction. Thus the operation of markets are seen as being more important than the potential consequences such as unemployment and homelessness. These consequences are seen as the result of natural predictive laws and thus unavoidable. Homelessness is seen as resulting not from market failure but because of cyclical adjustment or personal moral deficiencies. The problem is therefore that the Modern Conservatives have developed a description of the world out of a particular ideological prism. In effect the model predates any possible description with the latter consequently framed by the logic of the model.

However, it would not suffice merely to suggest replacing a Modern Conservative government with a social democrat or socialist one. Whilst the situation may improve in terms of funding in the public sector, the result would be merely to replace one example of modernity for another. It is the conceit of modernity, with its belief in competent and responsible government that I see as the main problem. The British Labour Party (which interestingly now declares itself as being "modernised") would maintain this conception of active government making centralised decisions about housing need, provision and access. The expectations of government right across the political spectrum lead almost inevitably to government as *the* responsible agent. Thus the most important point that can be derived from the discussion in Part One is that *unlimited government* is the housing problem.

Modernist housing policy, even on its own terms, is at its limits; it is at the very bounds of its sustainability. This situation goes beyond particular problems of finance and the mechanisms for distribution. It is not simply a case of increasing the funding to housing associations, or of allowing local authorities to build again. Rather we are faced with the question of the very manner in which housing policy is conceived, discussed and perceived. What I am concerned with here then is the very notion of a national housing policy as determinate and competent.

It should be clear, however, from the critique in Part One that this problematisation of government is not intended as an apologia for the New Right. However, nor am I content to accept the standard left wing discourses on the nature of housing policy. Much socialist discourse is like Modern Conservatism in being dependent upon modernist metanarratives and thus policies based on these discourses would be prey to the same criticisms I have presented in Part One. Both forms of discourse are prescriptive and collectivist and are content to use individuals as means to purported more worthwhile ends. In opposition to this I shall attempt to present a libertarian description that is antagonistic to Modern Conservatism *without* relying on what is the necessary determinism of socialism.

Indeed one of the more interesting, if disorienting, aspects of current political and social discourses is that the traditional labels of left and right no longer seem to apply so readily. Giddens (1994) has suggested that it is the right who are now seen, and see themselves, as the radical reformers changing a tired and worn out system. Moreover it is the parties of the left who find themselves defending the status quo of universal welfare provision. Commentators such as Gray (1993) and Taylor (1991) have also sought to address this apparent transformation. Taylor in particular has sought to show some of the apparent contradictions, or "cross alignments" (1991, p. 95) that makes political definition increasingly difficult:

> Right-wing American-style conservatives speak as advocates of traditional communities when they attack abortion on demand and pornography; but in their economic policies they advocate an untamed form of capitalist enterprise, which more than anything else

has helped to dissolve historic communities, has fostered atomism, which knows no frontiers or loyalties, and is ready to close a mining town or savage a forest habitat at the drop of a balance sheet. On the other side, we find supporters of an attentive, reverential stance to nature, who would go to the wall to defend the forest habitat, demonstrating in favour of abortion on demand, on the grounds that a woman's body belongs exclusively to her. Some adversaries of savage capitalism carry possessive individualism farther than its most untroubled defenders. (1991, p.95)

Of course, this is not to denigrate the seriousness with which each side maintains its position. It is rather to suggest that we should be cautious of using the labels "left" and "right" to dismiss a discourse without engaging with it. Thus whilst this discourse derives from a libertarian perspective, it does so within a spirit of pluralism whereby I am prepared to adopt and adapt elements from various discourses to develop my philosophical description. Whether it is seen as originating from the left, the centre or the right is a matter for the interpretation of others.

A spirit of pluralism is indeed what underlies the alternative framework for housing policy that is to be presented in Part Three of this essay. But there is more groundwork needed before I can attempt to put together even a tentative framework. In particular I seek to explore the limits of discourse about housing policy — of what it is that housing policy is presumed to be able to do. I shall undertake this examination by looking at three areas. Firstly, in this chapter, I shall present a critique of the means that are presumed to be available to the state in its policy making role. I shall aim to suggest that there are limits to this role, but that modernist institutions fail to appreciate where these boundaries lie. I shall thus look at some of the presuppositions that modernity has about the role of the state and go on to present an alternative model that recognises the division between the private and the public. This chapter will be more concerned with a general philosophical critique than a discussion of housing policy as such. However, it is only through a deconstruction of the political philosophy of modernity that the aporias at the heart of modernist policy making itself will be made manifest.

The second area I shall explore, in Chapter Five, is modernity's characterisation of the ends of policy, in particular with regard to the notions of rights and needs. I shall be particularly concerned to undermine discourses that present rights as natural and needs as universal. This critique will allow me to concentrate on how needs are fulfilled and who defines the means of fulfilment and indeed what the needs (and thus the ends of policy) themselves are. Thus Chapter Six examines an alternative means to fulfilment which is predicated on a different philosophical tradition to modernist rational discourse. This alternative housing process is one that concentrates on the implicit rather than the reasoned; on the self created instead of the received; and, on the vernacular instead of the modern. Thus Part Two of this essay is concerned to take us beyond a critique of modernist housing policy and into its philosophical underpinnings before going on to present a more sustainable alternative. I shall begin this discourse by examining the notion of limits.

4.1. The Ambiguity of Limits

Perhaps somewhat belatedly the title chosen for this book needs some explanation (the reason for its lateness is the desire to present a description of Modern Conservatism as near to its own terms as it is possible for an avowed sceptic of modernity to do). What does it mean to use the term, "limits of housing policy"? Is it a description of *what is* — of the extent of current policy — or of *what ought to be* — of what the extent of policy should be? Moreover, is it a reference to what is possessed by housing policy, in the sense that they are housing's limits, or alternatively to what controls housing? There are thus certain ambiguities in the term I have chosen as the banner headline for my descriptions of housing.

I would suggest that there are at least five ways in which the term 'limit' is used. Firstly, a limit can be seen as the ultimate degree or amount of a process or thing. It is to take something to its ultimate extent or breaking point. In terms of housing policy this notion of limit could be seen as the point at which it can go no further; it is where the policy is at breaking point, or where it terminates. Thus in this sense the limit refers to the point beyond which housing policy ceases to operate or even to exist. However, the sense of the term ultimately carries with it the connotation of persistence and resilience, of policy carrying on to the bitter end, where regardless of failure and disappointment the policy is persisted with to its conclusion. It is to suggest or to believe that there is no alternative and this will be justified by the ends of policy.

Secondly, the terms limits can be used to denote a boundary or edge of something. Thus the limits of housing policy can be seen as the boundary which terminates it, yet keeps it separate from other areas of policies. This sense of a boundary could also refer to the extremities in the sense of our being at the *outer limits* of policy. Thus one could refer to arguments and discourse that are extreme and thus at the very limit of acceptability. It would be a housing policy that is beyond the mainstream of established discourse.

Thirdly, the term can refer to the largest quantity or amount allowed; it is the ceiling or maximum placed around something that delimits the possibility of policy. This could be a constitutional limitation, a financial restriction or whatever. A limit in this sense is a *proscription* which sets the bounds of policy. The fourth use of the term is related in that it is where the term is used as a verb — to limit — that thus creates the proscription. It is where something is restricted, confined or demarcated. Furthermore it is to specify what is possible and what is not and thus restrict what policy may achieve.

The fifth use of the term is to refer to a person or thing that is intolerable or exasperating — it is *the limit*. It is something beyond which we cannot endure — *the last straw*. In this sense one could see that my title is referring to the intolerable nature of current housing policy; that modernist housing policy is just *the limit*.

Therefore the term can be used with a number of meanings, which are to an extent related, but which give different emphases and nuances to the discussion. I have suggested that current housing policy is unsustainable and that there is a potential breaking point where the contradictions of policy can no longer be reconciled — that modernist housing policy is at its limits. I have implied that such a situation is intolerable both in terms of the effects of policy and for the seriousness of academic discourses.

However, this is the not the primary sense in which I which to apply the term. My interest is in *limiting* housing policy; of suggesting what are the boundaries which should restrict and circumscribe the activity of policy makers. It is my aim to place a limitation around housing policy in order to make it tolerable and to ensure it is sustainable. Thus I am using the term to refer to the proscription of policy makers and agents, of setting limits to what they *may* do (Turner, 1976).

Such a definition — one that seeks to place restrictions rather than detail options and possibilities — appears to run counter to our avowed libertarianism. I am aware that I appear to be suggesting that the way to create a libertarian housing policy is by placing restrictions on what it is possible to do. This could be seen as being illiberal and thus opening myself up to the same sort of criticism that has been levelled at the Modern Conservatives, namely that my aims and methods of achieving them are contradictory.

However, I would suggest that this would be to conflate means with ends, which is precisely the problem with the rhetoric of the Modern Conservatives. They have seen it as their role — or rather the role of government — to liberate the individual from government interference. Thus they have interfered in the lives of individuals to remove this very interference. It is as if the avowed ends of their policy legitimate the means, whilst in fact the means actually undermine those ends. The Modern Conservatives create *lines* which the individual *must* follow, in the manner in which a train must follow the track in front of it. In short, they are prescribing the limits of the dwelling process.

My notion of limits is rather to suggest that the ends of policy may only be served by prescribing the limits within which institutions and individuals may act. It is to place constraints on the means of fulfilling personal ends, rather than to prescribe the ends themselves. I am thus separating means from ends. This is on the premise that our ends should be freely determined and this is only possible by placing restrictions on our and others' means of achieving them so as to ensure we do not coerce others into accepting our ends as their own. Thus I am not attempting to state what we must do, but rather what we may not, in order to give others the space to determine their own ends. This use of limits is thus a *negative* one, but it is necessarily so to permit our search for an anti-essentialist framework in which to place housing policy. It assumes no particular generalised outcome, but rather merely places restrictions on how outcomes may be pursued in order to preserve the diversity of personally defined outcomes. However, having now stated what it is I are referring to, I must now justify why I see it as an important distinction.

4.2. Negative Freedom

The definition of limits which I have chosen to employ rests upon one of the standard notions of contemporary liberal and libertarian thought, namely that of negative freedom. It is this notion, which permits the spontaneous market order to operate, that serves as the cornerstone of Hayek's (1960, 1982) economic liberalism, as well as being implicit within the libertarianism of Nozick (1974). However, I have already severely criticised Hayek and, furthermore, suggested that there are problems with Nozick's notion of the minimal state which derives its moral legitimacy from the freedom from coercion demanded by the negative definition of freedom. Therefore, if there are these reservations about the uses to which negative freedom, why do I insist upon its usefulness?

I can answer this question by making some brief comments about the ways in which both Hayek and Nozick use the concept of negative freedom. Gray (1995) suggests that the dominant schools of both historical and contemporary liberal thought have relied on a conception of rational choice. He includes the liberalism of Hayek, with its notion of the rational economic actor, and Nozick, with his view of the individual seeking to protect his/her inviolable rights, in this rationalist tradition. This rationality implies that there is a generally applicable set of criteria that will determine the actions of individuals within certain situations. This is a form of monism which supposes that all individual actions are ultimately reducible to a set of universal criteria or "laws", in the case of Nozick to particular moral rights. The crucial problem with any notion of human rationality is to suggest how this can be combined with the indeterminacy of liberalism as expressed by Hayek's spontaneous order created by free decision makers or Nozick's non-patterned principle. Indeed I have already offered Nozick's critique of Hayek who he sees as presenting a patterned principle based upon mutual economic benefit despite the latter's intentions. One could venture to suggest that Nozick himself may be creating a patterned principle through overstating entitlement as a rationally determined ordering mechanism. Thus, in both cases, the appeal to a universal rationality presents problems for the coherence of their avowed non-determinism.

Gray (1995) contrasts this form of rationally based liberalism with what he terms the "agonistic liberalism"(p. 1) of Berlin. This is a form of liberalism where "the value of freedom derives from the limits of rational choice" (p. 8). According to Gray, Berlin's liberalism is one of "conflict among inherently rivalrous goods" (p. 8), where we are presented with incommensurable choices with nothing beneath them to help us to adjudicate between them. There is no metaphysical foundation of rationality which underpins our decision making. The choices that we have to make are often irreconcilable and thus cannot be conflated by reference to any universal theory. It is also a view that rejects any notion of a common human nature. Berlin's, liberalism, as mediated by Gray into the concept of agonistic liberalism, appears to offer a radical, anti-essentialist alternative to the liberalism that underpins the Modern Conservatives and it is worthwhile therefore to pursue it further, particularly in our attempt to justify our negative concept of limits.

Berlin's essay entitled "Two Concepts of Liberty" (1969) is perhaps his most significant attempt to expound his brand of anti-essentialist liberalism. These two concepts are defined as *positive* and *negative* freedom. Positive freedom is the attempt to prescribe what liberties we have, whilst negative freedom proscribes what we cannot do to others. The former can be seen to actually limit freedom itself, whilst the latter allows for its greatest expression by limiting coercion from external sources. So far I have described the two concepts in a manner that would be acceptable to most liberals and libertarians. However, it is how Berlin extends the notions that creates their distinction from the economism of Hayek.

According to Berlin it is the concept of positive freedom that lies at the heart of the metaphysical foundations of the various totalising political ideologies. He defines positive freedom as the wish to be in control of our lives, rather than being at the mercy of external forces. It is to ask the question, "what am I free to do or be?" (1969, p. 130). An individual is concerned with exploring and extending the possibilities of his or her self-motivated actions. Thus it is where motivation is internal and proactive. We are not merely responding or reacting to stimuli from external agencies and other individuals. Rather, it is where power appears to be centred in the individual. One would have thought therefore that such a concept ought to be useful in defining individual agency and possibility.

The problem with this notion is that of the assumption of objective rationality. According to Kant (1990), freedom can only be attained with pure rationality where we are untainted by personal desire or inclination. It is where we act on the basis of universal abstract principles of rationality (Lindley, 1986). Kant's description leads us to a position where humans are seen as having a "real self" that is definitive and universal. Berlin states that it is but a short step from this position for thinkers to claim that they have discovered just what this "real self" is. Thus positive freedom leads to the position of the intellectual assuming an understanding of what is best for all others who are not so aware. The majority — not being intellectuals — may not be as conscious of their "real selves" and thus should be "encouraged" to find it. Of course, what differs across a variety of thinkers is what the "real self" is deemed to be.

Thus the consequence of positive freedom is that it leads to authoritarianism and a lack of personally defined freedom. Berlin succinctly describes this development from individual freedom to authoritarian direction:

> ... first, that all men have one true purpose, and one only, that of rational self-direction; second, that the ends of all rational beings must of necessity fit into a single universal, harmonious pattern, which some men may be able to discern more clearly than others; third, that

all conflicts, and consequently all tragedy, is due solely to the clash of
reason with the irrational or the insufficiently rational — the imma-
ture and undeveloped elements in life — whether individual or
communal, and that such clashes are, in principle, avoidable, and for
wholly rational beings impossible; finally, that when all men have
been made rational, they will obey the rational laws of their own na-
tures, which are one and the same in them all, and so be at once
wholly law-abiding and wholly free. (1969, p.154)

Berlin is thus suggesting that a view of freedom that puts possibility at
its centre will lead to authoritarianism because of the effect of a
dominant ideology, which acts as a focus for this possibility. The question "what am I free to do or be?" becomes "what must I do or be?"
One can agree with Berlin that there is no shortage of thinkers willing
to provide an answer.

Berlin contrasts this positive conception with a description of negative freedom. This he describes as "liberty from" as opposed to "liberty
to" (1969, p. 127). Berlin describes this as the situation where persons
are protected from coercion and are thus able to pursue their individual
aims and objectives; it is the "warding off of interference" (p. 127).
Gray (1995) defines Berlin's concept as "choice among alternatives or
options that is unimpeded by others" (p. 15). This more nuanced definition is important for two reasons. Firstly, it explicitly states the notion
of choice — it is freedom to choose, and not the "freedom" to be the
sort of person that Hayek or the Modern Conservatives take us to be.
Secondly, it clears up a misunderstanding of Haworth (1994), who suggests that Berlin's definition implies that we are not free if a road is
blocked off several hundred miles away from where we live and thus
which we have no use for. Haworth thus contends that Berlin is concerned with the ability to be free rather than the capability of acting
freely. However, Gray's definition is one of choice between alternatives
or options which need not be exhaustive. We need not deliberate over
every possibility, merely those that are presented before us. It is the
choice that is unimpeded not the alternatives or options.

The significance of this definition of negative freedom is that there
is no desired end-state or purpose for liberty, and most certainly it is

not an end in itself. Berlin criticises other conceptions of liberty that do not "allow for the variety of basic human needs" (1969, p. 162). As I have suggested, thinkers and politicians concern themselves with a narrow parameter of priorities and tend to ignore those concerns which are inconvenient or fail to fit into their system. Thus the Modern Conservatives have residualised public renting because it does not fit into their model of how free agents should behave.

Berlin suggests that human society is not so directed. Human ends are different and diverse, and therefore a single all-embracing system is neither possible nor desirable. If we accept the primacy of the individual we must accept also that a society is pluralist and this, Berlin suggests, entails negative freedom where the aims and objectives of individuals are protected. This "value pluralism" (Gray, 1995, p. 1) implies that there can be no appeal to any natural law or set of principles which underwrites all of human existence.

However, some form of limitation is necessary if individuals are to be free of interference and able to make unimpeded choices. Such a society must develop what Berlin calls "frontiers of freedom" (1969, p. 165) over which on one may not cross. These cultural norms or standards may be termed differently — natural rights, the word of God or whatever — but they must be "widely grounded" (p. 165) so as to be accepted as natural. These frontiers or limits are, however, contingent upon the particular community. They offer a frame of reference and limitation, but they are relative notions, not a natural grounding.

Such frontiers (or limits) are necessary because the divergent aims of human beings are by no means compatible and therefore conflict is not only possible, but inevitable. This very incommensurability, however, ensures that it is not possible to create an overarching scale or system of values. We cannot fall back upon eternally valid principles in order to resolve disputes, but rather we must rely on negotiation within the agreed limits. A system of values does not then become a tool of coercion, nor does it merely mirror a dominant ideology.

This perspective is an individualistic, pluralistic one that begins to recognise contingency as a prerequisite for freedom. It is where:

... the ideal of freedom to choose ends without claiming eternal
validity for them, and the pluralism of values connected with this...
(Berlin, 1969, p. 172)

This description of liberalism places individuals at its centre, but
proposes no specific purpose to them other than that which is self-
determined. Thus individuals are empowered through their ability to
create their own purpose free from external constraints. Individual
agency in this sense is more real despite its derivation from a structure
of limits. In addition there is an emergent recognition that there are no
eternal values, or totalising visions, merely a cocktail of contingent
possibilities. It can be distinguished from Hayek's concept by this contingency and belief in the incommensurability of human purposes.
Thus a concept of negative freedom derived from the work of Berlin
and Gray helps to justify my concern for limits within policy
making. What I need now to pursue is how this anti-essentialism appears within the social or public context. I need to describe the
relationship between the unimpeded choices of the individual and
the agreed frontiers of that freedom. Housing policy, despite its
private consequences, implies the use of public resources which is
decided through some form of public discourse. How this can be
achieved is my next concern.

4.3. Limits to Public Policy

One of the problems of any description of libertarianism is to find a
means of linking the personal with the public — of linking individual
and social action together in a way that does not deny the incommensurability of means and ends that I have suggested are so important in
any description of negative liberty. As a community we are limited in
our ability to suggest the imposition of a particular solution. However,
if this is the case, how is social adhesion possible? Is it possible to suggest a way that protects individual possibility within a framework of
solidarity? Put another way, is it possible to present a non-patterned
description of the social world? The purpose of this section is to suggest that such a description can be developed through a critical reading
of the *liberal ironism* of Rorty (1989; 1991a; 1991b). I shall show that

Rorty's description offers itself as a useful tool for the resolution of the dichotomy between public and private action.

Rorty has attempted to provide what he refers to as a reformulation of "the hopes of liberal society in a non-rationalist and non-universalist way" (1989, p.44). He therefore, like Berlin, rejects the search for a metaphysical foundation to a community. But, in so doing, he has explicitly addressed the issue of equating the public with the private. These two spheres should be separated; that our private purposes should be distinguished from our public purposes and thus not seen as within the legitimate ambit of public policy.

Rorty begins by building up a picture of the individual and his or her moral environment, building upon the philosophy of the later Wittgenstein and Davidson. He suggests that "all human beings carry about a set of words which they employ to justify their actions, their beliefs, and their lives" (1989, p. 73). This Rorty terms an individual's *final vocabulary*. He sees it as final in the sense that when pressed the individual has no recourse to a non-circular argument; there is nothing beneath it to which we can appeal for its justification. It is final in a moral rather than a temporal sense — it is not where we may end up, but rather where we are emphatically now. Our final vocabulary is thus in effect our personal morality.

Our personal final vocabulary imbues the world with meaning for us, rather than necessarily linking us to an external reality. Indeed, there are no external standards or forms to which an individual can "measure" moral and ethical issues. This implies that it is impossible for us to conceive of a community called "humanity" which has its own intrinsic nature. There is no common human nature that behaviour is predicated upon. Rorty is concerned to shift the description of liberalism:

> ... to a society conceived as a band of eccentrics collaborating for purposes of mutual protection rather than as a band of fellow spirits united by a common goal. (1989, p.59)

Individuals do not come together because of any common nature or set of immutable laws giving a grounding to a particular society. Instead Rorty moves towards a form of privatised existence — "a band of eccentrics", individuated and self referenced — combined through a solidarity that depends upon this distinctiveness. He describes this notion as liberal ironism and he sees it as a form of existence where people combine their commitment to a moral framework — their final vocabulary — "with a sense of the contingency of their commitment" (1989, p. 61).

We have a final vocabulary that is the basis of our moral existence, yet this is not an inviolable, natural or immutably grounded foundation — they are not a collection of natural rights. We are rather in a contingent, relational state that may change as we encounter new experiences and circumstances. Rorty describes a liberal society as being about such fresh and open encounters rather than being based on temporal foundations. There is thus no prior order that overrides any final vocabulary. Instead "a liberal society is one which is content to call "true" whatever the upshot of such encounters turn out to be" (1989, p. 52).

A liberal ironist is one who is prepared to accept these outcomes as "true" and therefore reject their old final vocabulary for one that is more current. This position is an anti-essentialist one in that truth is determined by no pre-ordained schema, but rather through free encounters.

Rorty's position appears to be useful in our search for a non-patterned libertarianism in that it leads to the view that the significant process of a libertarian society is that of public discussion. It is through public discussion that private interests come together into the public sphere. Individuals are attracted to each other by certain common elements in their final vocabularies. They are able to understand and, importantly, to agree with each other. However, the nature of this public discussion is limited. It would centre upon two questions, firstly, such discussion would concern itself with "how to balance the needs for peace, wealth and freedom, when conditions require that one of these goals be sacrificed to one of the others", and secondly, "how to equalise opportunities for self creation and then leave people alone to use or neglect their opportunities" (1989, p. 84).

One could redescribe Rorty's statement by suggesting that a community comes together to derive the limits that allow for individuals to take advantage of the alternatives before them without being impeded by others. The community comes together to devise the frontiers for freedom. These frontiers are defined negatively as protecting the opportunities for self creation.

Rorty believes that "this is all the social glue liberal societies need" (1989; p. 84). A society needs open encounters on those issues that may impose relationships within a community. It can provide these open encounters by equalising opportunities for self creation — by offering individuals the tools with which to shape themselves — but that is all it should do. It should not dictate the outcomes of these encounters, nor should it presume that any encounter is true in any representational sense. There can be no encounter that delivers the "final" outcome. One encounter may be more significant than others, but not to the extent that it curtails future encounters.

This implies that a libertarian society is not bound together by philosophical beliefs. Instead of any metaphysical foundation, Rorty suggests that "what binds societies together are common vocabularies and common hopes" (1989; p.86). We come together because of the possibility of agreement and the understandability implicit within that possibility. Rorty sees this as an ethical, rather than an epistemological or metaphysical base.

This ethical base is not a universalistic one, but one based on our own perception of danger and hope — of the consequences of cruelty. This is the root of solidarity in a libertarian society. We are prepared to endanger ourselves for another, not as critics of Rorty such as Elshtain (1992) have suggested, out of any claim to universal human solidarity, but because we share, or can envisage sharing, their predicament. Indeed as Bauman (1989) has suggested, in the most extreme case of the century, it was lack of human contact — or open dialogue — which led to the seemingly ready acceptance of the mass annihilation of European Jews. According to Bauman, it was because Germans and Poles did not have Jews as neighbours that the holocaust became a possibility. Bauman's point is that it is harder to demonise those who live amongst us. Thus solidarity arises out of the recognition of shared possibility and the consequences of its loss.

It is not necessary in a society based upon open dialogue for there to be shared beliefs. Individuals do not need to agree to common aims based on foundational principles. We may pursue our aims free from interference. We may use our opportunities for self creation as we wish, including squandering them or leaving them idle. Indeed shared beliefs would limit the infinite variety of private self creation (Hall, 1994). Individual action need only be modified if it leads to public action — i.e., that impinges on the needs for peace, wealth and freedom — which cannot be justified to most of our fellow citizens. Put another way this is where we come up against the frontiers of freedom which serve to protect ourselves and others from coercion.

This connection between negative freedom and solidarity offers a means of bringing libertarianism and social solidarity together into dialogue. I have attempted to maintain the incommensurability of human beliefs and ends, yet without neglecting solidarity. I have thus sought to put together an anti-essentialist description of a community of separated individuals who share possibilities and experience through contact and dialogue in a common environment without presuming a particular set of outcomes. I have tried to show that what is important is the nature of the processes involved to achieve outcomes, and how these allow for freedom and the possibility for self creation. It should, however, be clear that solidarity is the condition of protecting freedom and is thus to be seen as derivative of it. In other words our libertarianism is the prior condition.

This description of a libertarian community has far reaching consequences for housing policy. The most important of which is to suggest that policy must be decided locally by those who are to use and benefit from it. It implies that any policy can only provide the framework for individual choice — policy, as shall see, is what makes choice effective.

A further significant point that comes out of this description is that the role of housing in a libertarian community is distinct from that in a society dictated by modernist principles. It takes us beyond modernity's characterisation of the means of fulfilment, and thus the purpose of policy. Instead of policy being determined by a totalising vision of the purpose of housing, we should see the dwelling as a place in which the infinite variety of human ends can be expressed free from interference. Housing is experienced by households, and it therefore falls within the sphere of private action. We should see the dwelling as a boundary which separates public from private. This implies a different role for the state in policy making, and furthermore, a different role for discourse about the role of the state and its interventions in the housing process.

This implies the operation of limits at two distinct, but inter-related levels. Firstly, in terms of the protection of the autonomy and needs of the individual users in their dwelling. There must be limits set upon the ways in which their home environment can be interfered with. Secondly, we must place limits on the process of housing to ensure that the means of provision do not subsume the ends of the users. This is an issue of the control of the process and I shall show that it is only through the control of the process that the integrity of individual ends can be guaranteed. However, I shall first explore the nature of human autonomy and needs which this process can serve. In doing so I shall present a detailed critique of the universalistic description of the ends of policy presented by modernist discourses.

CHAPTER FIVE

AUTONOMY, RIGHTS AND HOUSING NEED

The Modern Conservatives attempted to place the individual at the centre of their housing policy. Their rhetoric stressed the need for personal responsibility and individual choice. This rhetoric is summed up in the title of the 1995 White Paper, *Our Future Homes: Opportunity, Choice and Responsibility* (DOE, 1995b). This makes the aims of Modern Conservatism explicit and is further emphasised by the opening words of the foreword to the White Paper written by the Secretary of State for the Environment:

> All over the industrial world, Governments are having to decide where the frontier should lie between the role of the State in providing for the necessities of life and the role of the individual in taking responsibility for meeting his or her own needs. (DOE, 1995, p. 3)

This quote shows both the contradiction at the heart of Modern Conservatism — "Governments are having to decide as the primary agent in the housing process. The difficulty, of course, is that the flaw in Modern Conservative ideology actually mitigates against individual choice through the imposition of centrally administered opportunities.

However, this problem in Modern Conservatism does not mean that a concern for the individual's role is misplaced. Indeed it is this emphasis by the Modern Conservatives that made their housing policy popular and readily acceptable to a majority throughout the 1980s. They were apparently attuned to the manner in which individual households see their housing as an expression of themselves. The unsustainability of the policy, and the consequent decline in its popularity, derived out of a particularly narrow understanding of this expression which concentrated on individuals as economic agents and not as carers, lovers and family members. Thus the success of the policy was guaranteed only so long as the economic conditions were able to support it.

The Modern Conservatives present a mere caricature of the complexity of the relationship between the dweller and the dwelling. In their economism they do not appreciate the notions of value, attachment and security that is given to the dwelling in its guise as home. Saunders (1990), in his attempt to show the benefits of owning above renting, suggests that owner occupiers have a greater sense of ontological security than tenants. He suggests that:

> ... we may suggest that home ownership is one expression of the search for ontological security, for a home of one's own offers both a physical (hence spatially rooted) and permanent (hence temporally rooted) location in the world. Our home is unambiguously a place where we belong, and the things that belong to us, and the things that we do there have an immediacy of presence and purpose...it may be suggested that home ownership represents an individual solution to the problem of alienation. (1990, p. 293)

Owners are seen as being more able to "be themselves" (p. 302) because they see their home as a place where they can relax. They experience greater autonomy than renters as a result of the choices that are open to them as owners. This is to suggest that security derives from property rights.

The paucity of this position can be shown by the history of the books publication. It was researched in 1985-86 during a period of appreciating house prices and was published in 1990 at the top of the Lawson boom. Saunders was thus able to present a picture of the housing market as offering security. Yet, as the subsequent depression in the housing market proved, this security was an illusion based on a simplistic notion of the meaning and use of home.

Thus security relies on more than ownership. Indeed Gurney (1990), in his study on the affective nature of the home, has shown:

> Instead of people's housing tenure being the cause of widespread feelings of niche and belonging at home, it is merely that most (not all) people experience their home as a happy place where loving relationships between kin and non-kin relations most often take place, and as a place full of memories and charged with meaning. (p. 26)

He goes on:

> The individual's concept of home is based on layer upon layer of intensely personal experiences ... These intensely personal experiences mean that home is a familiar, welcoming place full of memories and meanings. This is the real source of security that can be derived from the home. (p. 26)

The home is a network of past and present relationships marked by intimacy. Property relations are mediated by this network and not the reverse. This means that a council tenant may be as secure as an owner occupier. Tenure is not the determining factor. Indeed, Gurney seems to suggest that the meaning of the home may only be personally expressed — we can say what our home means to us, but this may not concur with others. In short it may not be possible to generalise without the risk of caricature and over-simplification.

However, my concern is not to pursue the debate about the meaning of the home, but rather to use this example to suggest that modernist discourses have ignored what is elemental to the experience of the dwelling process. The concern with material aggregations of dwellings ignores how we live as emotional and vulnerable beings within private relationships. I rather seek to outline the manner in which individuals may play a part in the housing process. I am concerned with how households may seek to control the process, not with what particular parts or the results of the process mean to them. This does not imply that the debate on the meaning of the home is not important, but rather that it is such a subtle and complex area of research has been ignored in policy making. Of course, the descriptions in this chapter are related to the debate on the home in that they attempt to build up a notion of the individual's relation to the housing process. But the concern is only on what could be called the *political relation* of control of the housing proces rather than dealing with the territorial, psychological and phenomenological aspects that go along with this political relation (see Depres, 1991 and Somerville, 1993 for comprehensive reviews of the literature on the home).

My concern, in concentrating on the politics of control, will instead look at three issues that can be seen as central to the construction of the individual. Firstly, I shall briefly explore the notion of autonomy and attempt to redescribe it in relativist terms. Secondly, and as part of our description of autonomy, I shall reject the notion of rights as a focus for policy, and thirdly, I shall discuss the issue of needs. Modernity has attempted to develop universal ends to which we should all apparently aim to attain. Thus policies are sought to satisfy those needs which we all share as humans. In criticising this notion I shall propose a relativity of need that will allow me to propose a vernacular housing process in which autonomous individuals can operate.

5.1. Autonomy and Rights

My description of libertarianism denies the need for a foundational base to a community. There is no external criteria with which to judge opposing values or final vocabularies. This denies one of the central aims of modernity which was to create order predicated upon universal and immutable qualities that define as us human (Bauman, 1991). The dominant quality was seen as the ability to reason and thus we were separated from the animals ruled solely by their passions and desires. The particular effect of this libertarian description is to reject this concept of rationality.

Kant (1990) believed that humans are only truly free when they are acting as fully rational agents. This is a condition where they are "motivated by purely rational principles which are untainted by particular inclinations or interests" (Lindley, 1986; p. 20). We are free only when we deny our animal passions and desires. Lindley states that "such purity requires that one act only on principles one is prepared to universalise in a strong sense" (1986; p. 20). Rationality is seen as an ideal to which each human being has the possibility of attaining. This concept of Kantian rationality thus leads to the concept of a universal human nature. We have a particular essence by virtue of being a rational human being.

My libertarian description, built on the work of Berlin and Rorty, sees such a concept of rationality as ludicrous. There can be no claims to justice outside of a particular community with its discrete culture, history and traditions built up by public dialogue. A non-circular argument in defence of universal justice is ultimately not a credible possibility.

What I can offer instead is a redescription of the concept of autonomy which does away with the assumption of rationality. This conception can be clearly demonstrated through a critique of the linkage between rational autonomy and rights.

Conventional conceptions of autonomy, underpinned by the assumption of rationality, lead into a discourse on natural rights. I have sought to show this relation in operation in my discussion of Modern Conservatism. Individuals are seen to have economic and property rights that derive out of a particular patterned principle of justice. This in turn is based on an assumption of the "true" human essence. Social democracy likewise, with its stress on political, civil and social rights, is imbued with a concept of the rational human agent who has certain rights which fulfil citizens as ends in themselves. All such conceptions of autonomy assume a particular essence with a rational core.

Lindley offers a definition of autonomy which states this rational condition strongly:

> To be autonomous requires ... that one have a developed self to which one's actions can be ascribed. This in turn requires a consciousness of oneself as a being who acts for reasons, whose behaviour can be explained by reference to one's own goals and purposes. (1986; p. 6)

The autonomous person is one who has a conscious will and purpose. Furthermore, this purpose can be objectively stated. Doyal and Gough (1991) define autonomy in a similar way, but with an even greater emphasis on rationality. According to them, to be autonomous is:

> ... to have the ability to make informed choices about what should be done and how to go about doing it. This entails being able to formulate aims, and beliefs about how to achieve them, along with the ability to evaluate the success of these beliefs in the light of empirical evidence. (1991; p. 53)

This definition of autonomy not only states that an individual has an objective purpose, but has also the ability for critical evaluation. Autonomy, according to Doyal and Gough, appears to involve a form of calculating cost-benefit analysis of our goals.

Kemeny demonstrates this typology of the rational maximiser when he discusses the relationship between the household and the locality:

> Households acquire a dwelling with a view to match existing and projected household budgets and the life cycle space needs, and to harmonise and compromise between sometimes conflicting priorities of household members concerning space and facility needs. (1992a, p. 11)

Households are seen as holding a particular purpose in mind in taking decisions, and it is implicit in Kemeny's description that this purpose can be generalised.

The danger implicit in these definitions is that it begs the question of "what one is (objectively) free to do or be?" (Berlin, 1969). There can be, of course, only one "answer" to this question as (objectively) objectivity cannot be either plural or contingent. Objectivity is definitive and incontrovertible. Kukathas (1992) clearly outlines the nature of this danger:

> The ideal of autonomy is the ideal of the intellectual. It is the ideal of those who stress the importance of our rational faculties: our capacity to reflect, to deliberate, to choose. (1992; p. 108)

He goes on:

> The upholder of autonomy often forgets that people are too busy living their lives to worry about directing it, too often he remembers, and exercises his ingenuity looking for ways of forcing them to be autonomous. At worst, this involves doing violence to the actual practices and lives people pursue; at best it means paternalistic action to "create the conditions" which make autonomy possible

Kukathas is here echoing Berlin's criticism of positive freedom whereby the intellectual seeks to direct individuals towards a consciousness of their "true selves". However, he is also suggesting that autonomy, as defined by Doyal and Gough and Kemeny, is not a central concern of individuals. He suggests that we are too actively engaged in pursuing our goals to sit back and quantify, to question and evaluate them. This relates to my description of public discussion as the focus of the public sphere, whereby individuals engage with the community in a subjective manner, rather than in a universally prescribed objective way. This, as I have shown, is to differentiate between private and public action. The Kantian conception of autonomy, however, implies that the public describes the private will. Indeed there is no private will that is not given by the universal public will. It is where a totalising human essence determines our private actions.

A description of autonomy based on our anti-essentialist principles would be radically different. Firstly, I would not seek to deny the notion of rationality altogether. Whilst there is no objective human rationality, one can still suggest that individuals are able to act rationally in the sense of making decisions that most favour and accord with their own values and needs. We are able to make ourselves, at least partly, from the inside (Gray, 1995).

As individuals we radiate outwards into the community through the boundary of our private selves. We encounter the world via our description of ourselves moderated by the traditions, history and culture of our community. Indeed, community and solidarity are expressions of the recognition of the similarities of meaning within the values and vocabularies of others, not the commonality of the values and vocabularies themselves.

We are autonomous because of our ability for self description. Thus to use our final vocabulary is to exercise our autonomy. Autonomy demonstrates the subjectivity of the individual rather than confirming a common objective humanity. Therefore, autonomy is freedom for personal agency and nothing more. In other words, it is freedom from manipulation by others. Thus it is where we are free to exercise choice unimpeded by others. There is no suggestion or conception of what should guide or determine that choice. That we are able to use this freedom is because we are autonomous, not a necessary condition for it.

Furthermore this description of autonomy shows our ability to connect our moral agency spatially and temporally as a distinctive individual within a community. It is where we are linked by shared descriptions within different personal vocabularies, yet it is the individual that comes to the community (and is thus able to withdraw from it) rather than the community defining the individual. It thus places a limit around the community, rather than the individual.

However, autonomy is not directed towards a purpose or aim. It is an implicit condition and not a conscious controlling and evaluative process. As Kukathas states we are "too busy living (our) lives to worry about directing it" (1992; p. 108).

This pluralist view of freedom is inconsistent with a theory of natural rights. If we have a natural essence — if we are acquisitive rational maximisers, as the Modern Conservatives suggest — then that implies we have the right to express that essence. If we are of a particular type, then we must act in accordance with it. Accordingly we should have the right to do so — we have the right to show our "true selves". Thus to claim a universal human nature is to claim particular universal rights. The Modern Conservatives call for the right to personal property is a means of facilitating individual economic action determined by our essential rationality.

However, to describe a contingent, non-patterned society is to suggest that there is no such essence and therefore there can be no universal rights which we enjoy as a result of that essential nature. All such a society may have are legal constructs aimed at protecting the agreed freedoms within a society. These may be termed rights — and indeed often are — but we should see them rather as contingent, historically bound "frontiers of freedom" (Berlin, 1969; p. 165). These are the mechanisms that seek "to equalise opportunities for self creation" (Rorty, 1989, p. 84) and which should then leave us to use or neglect these opportunities. These frontiers, therefore only have a validity determined by their agreed acceptability within the community. Thus the "rights" of the unborn can be removed through legislation and periodically reviewed when the community believes the current position is wrong. The community may impose greater restrictions on abortion because of the improved chances of survival of premature babies.

This conclusion has implications for the framing of policy. If there is no external criteria by which to measure human action, how are we able to determine, for example, what housing is necessary for a community, except in terms of bare quantity? On what basis is a community to determine those facilities and action that are deemed to be desirable? Such problems are not avoided merely by a restatement of this problem in terms of the individual as the Modern Conservatives have sought to do. We, as individuals, are faced with the same qualitative dilemma as a group of individuals together. We can neither talk of the rights of a community, nor the rights of an individual. Thus to talk of the right to housing or shelter is misplaced, as it is to suggest we have the right to a certain standard of living or amenity. There is no human essence that demands that certain facilities be provided. This also implies that there is no respondent duty on any individual or agency to meet these demands.

But if the vocabulary of rights is deficient, how are we able to express our solidarity with others in our community? Moreover how can we be seen as being in any sense free? Rorty's work can again help here. Solidarity arises out of a shared recognition of the potential for loss; of the consequences of the central facets of our lives being humiliated — of an enforced redescription cruelly depriving us of the immediate certainty of our taken for granted world:

> ... human solidarity is not a matter of sharing a common truth or a common goal but of sharing a common selfish hope, the hope that one's world — the little things around which one has woven into one's final vocabulary — will not be destroyed. (1989, p. 92)

Through identifying what is important to ourselves, and recognising the pain of their potential loss, we are able to recognise that this pain is a possibility for others. Our solidarity is based around this possibility, and our public dialogue is an attempt to extend our abilities in recognising the important "little things" in the worlds of others. We are able to be outward looking because of the security of our own environment, and we realise that this is only a possibility because our environment is protected through the solidarity of the community. Thus we need the community for our autonomy, and in turn our autonomy allows us to continue this mutual support.

Rorty's description is of use to us as it can be reframed into one of needs. The important little things are those which fulfil our needs both in the material and ontological senses. I would thus suggest that solidarity and autonomy depends upon needs rather than rights. This allows us to attend directly with the circumstances of our particular individual or community and how they can be met on their own terms, instead of a discourse of rights which is dependent on universal categories of human nature and which can only be determined by the response of those deemed to have the duty to fulfil rights. As I have shown with the Modern Conservatives, they have taken on the role of both defining the rights of the individual and determining how they should be fulfilled. A discourse based on needs will allow me to circumvent this modernist dilemma. But, before I am able to do so I shall have to dispel the tendency, within discourses inimicable to Modern Conservatism in particular, to universalise human need.

5.2. Needs

I have claimed that human beings do not have natural rights. There are no immutable, foundational principles that underpin our relations with each other. What are called "rights" are nothing more than contingent boundaries aimed at protecting individuals from interference. However, what are they contingent upon? What is it that determines the parameters for human relationships, as something must, even though they may not remain so permanently and under all circumstances?

I have suggested that it is encountering other final vocabularies that allows us to recognise the important aspects in another's lifeworld and thus for solidarity and the protection of others to develop. This can be seen as a redescription of the politics of human needs.

However, this is not to suggest a universality of needs. To do so would be merely to replace natural rights with needs in the attempt to define humanity. I shall rather define needs as relative and culturally and historically dependent. Our needs are determined within our vernacular context.

The debate about the nature of human needs is, of course, a complex one. It is a debate, however, that is often conducted in the language of the relativist/foundationalist divide. Those who describe a concept of universal human needs appear to base their description upon a metaphysical foundation. Opponents of this view, such as Berlin and Rorty, are prepared to rely on history, public discussion or solidarity based on shared hope. This debate can be seen as centring around the control of the means of fulfilment. Foundationalists or universalists suggest that they can define needs and the necessary level of fulfilment. A relativist position is one where fulfilment can only be defined by those who express the particular need. I shall explore this debate through a brief critique of a recent influential attempt to present a universal theory of human need by Doyal and Gough (1991).

They believe that a relativist concept of need has allowed for subjective needs to be subsumed into a vocabulary of market preferences and consumer choices. Their contention is that relativism has presented no effective opposition to the Modern Conservatives. Subjectivism does not pose any principled opposition to the ideology of individual economic maximisers.

In place of this supposedly ineffectual relativism, Doyal and Gough seek to construct a theory of basic human needs based around the "avoidance of serious harm" (1991; p. 50). They define "serious harm" as when we are being "fundamentally disabled in our pursuit of the good" (1991; p. 50). In order to achieve this condition two basic universal needs are seen as necessary. Firstly, we must have *personal autonomy* and I have already discussed their definition of this in my discussion of autonomy. I observed that it was a redescription of the Kantian notion of rational will, but with a particular emphasis on evaluation and calculation. The second basic human need is *physical survival and health*. Doyal and Gough see this as the ability to act or to carry out necessary actions. The loss of health or autonomy entails disablement and an inability to create or share in the good things of life however defined. They are thus presenting two universal needs that exist regardless of time, culture and tradition.

These two basic needs are met by a series of what they term *universal satisfiers*, such as food, water, housing and security. These are seen as being intermediate and derived from the two basic needs. We need food and water not for itself, but to maintain our health and avoid serious harm. Doyal and Gough state that these satisfiers are also universal as they are required in all cultures. However, these intermediate needs have only to be above a certain level to achieve satisfaction, with anything above that level being subjective and merely satisfying wants rather than needs.

Despite the seeming ubiquity and practicality of Doyal and Gough's theory there are a number of problems with it which invalidate its possible application. Firstly, I would suggest that their conception of rationality is deficient. Doyal and Gough define it as consisting of a cost-benefit analysis by the rational maximiser. Indeed, it is a conception that appears to be characteristic of the rational policy maker in a modern welfare state rather than of human beings in their generality.

Secondly, their conception of health is vague to the point of meaninglessness. What is the criteria that defines whether we are able to act or not? How is this to be determined in practice, and, of course, by whom? Are Doyal and Gough suggesting that there are some objective criteria for stating when an individual is able to act? If they are stating that it is merely physical survival that is necessary, in the sense that one is not clinically dead, then it appears to be a sufficient condition that life be maintained by artificial means in an intensive care unit. Yet this state offers only a limited conception of personal autonomy, and this is the third objection to Doyal and Gough's theory. Elements within their definitions of autonomy and health may contradict the other universal need. Indeed their conception of autonomy implies a considerable degree of physical and mental capacity that would almost certainly be beyond many persons with a mental or physical disability. We are portrayed as autonomous when we are able to make informed choices on what and how; to formulate strategies to achieve them; and then to be able to evaluate them in "the light of empirical evidence" (1991; p. 51) in order to make better informed choices in the future. This does not appear to be a basic condition, but rather it implies decision making skills of a high level.

The fourth criticism of Doyal and Gough's theory relates to their notion of intermediate satisfiers. They state that only a particular standard or level of these satisfiers are necessary and that provision over this level merely fulfils subjective wants. This raises two separate objections. Firstly, how do we objectively set a standard that separates basic need from subjective want? Doyal and Gough contend that basic needs are not culturally dependent, and therefore presumably not historically specific either (assuming that there is a link between cultural development and the history of that community). Therefore basic needs are portrayed as not changing across cultures or over time. In the case of housing, Doyal and Gough believe that it need be safe, warm, not over-crowded and with sanitation; everything else desired by a household would be subjective (1991; p. 162). This is taken to be universal, yet in how many cultures would it be taken as acceptable? If acceptability cannot be accounted for within a universal category I would suggest that it is of limited use to talk of such a category. We cannot expect households to ignore what they consider needs merely because they are redefined by others as desires and arbitrarily given a lower order of significance.

Doyal and Gough assume that concepts of warmth, safety and over-crowding can be defined in ways open to universalisation. They thus, for example, seem to be suggesting that there is an all encompassing notion of safety shared by all individuals regardless of time or culture. However, in reality safety is an intensely personal ontological and emotional concept immune to external determination. No external agent is able to convince us that we are safe because of some universal category. Moreover, warmth is relatively more or less important depending on climate, the use that the dwelling is asked to fulfil and the age and health of the occupants. It is not possible to state at what level warmth goes beyond a universal satisifier and becomes a mere fulfiller of subjective wants. It depends on whether we are discussing the needs of new-born babies, the elderly or an affluent couple with the financial ability to make "rational" decisions about energy use. No universal standard is possible here except to say that, generally, warmth is better than cold. Doyal and Gough are therefore not practically able to define standards that are anything but banalities.

The second criticism of Doyal and Gough's description of inter-mediate needs is that they ignore the effect of expectations on needs. If humans are not rational maximisers they will not seek to separate objective rational needs and subjective expectations (Doyal and Gough fail to offer any reason why individuals should give preference to the former). Any need will develop an expectation of fulfilment and it is not possible to separate one from the other. Indeed, they will tend to feed off each other in a circular process. Individuals have expectations about certain amenities they can expect to enjoy, e.g., in modern Britain, most households can expect to become owner occupiers. This will have an influence on their perceptions of what they feel they need. It is interesting that modern British politics now appears to turn on the creation and maintenance of the "feel good factor", which, if it means anything, is the subjective perception of whether our needs are being, or are likely to be, fulfilled. Thus in political terms, standards are as likely to be determined by expectations as the needs that they are conditioned by, and therefore they will be relative rather than absolute. Expectations are not constant, but rather alter because of external conditions, and these conditions are locally and historically specific. This is why policy making is seen as a process in need of constant attention rather than a matter of providing the correct answer that definitively solves the "problem" of social and political relations.

To provide a standard based on supposedly objective basic human needs would necessitate an external imposition based on universal criteria decided by those conscious of humanity's "true essence". Doyal and Gough's theory of need implies the imposition of a prescriptive set of standards of provision based on a particular view of human rationality.

In effect they are describing basic human needs in terms of the provision of *merit goods*. This implies an important assumption at the heart of Doyal and Gough's theory which is important to my critique of modernist housing policy. A merit good is one that is provided outside of the price mechanism on the basis of *merit* or *need*. This, of course begs the question as to who should decide on merit or need. It is clear within Doyal and Gough's theory (and in housing needs analyses I discuss below) that it is the role of government to define merit and need. The conventional position is to suggest that there will be an underprovision of merit goods if allocation is left to private individuals. This is because the effects of any externalities are not appreciated by the individual consumer with limited knowledge.

However, I wish to present an alternative description of need which denies that housing is a merit good and thus suggest that its provision is not a matter for government prescription. This alternative can be built up through the distinctive definitions of need as a lack and as a necessity.

Firstly, need can be described as a *lack of something*. This is where there is a deficiency of a particular property or condition. Need is seen here to relate to satisfaction. This may be an imperative condition in that its lack threatens life, yet it may equally be evidence of a want or desire. Thus an imperative state is not a defining characteristic of need as a lack. Need so defined does not necessarily imply a fundamental condition of existence.

Secondly, to define need as a *necessity* is to see it as a basic human requirement. It is something that is deemed necessary for human existence. It, of course, does not define humanity, but it rather makes human life itself possible and recognisable. Turner describes the position, in relation to housing, as being "existentially significant" (1972; p. 153).

These necessities are not however, merely restricted to functional, biological needs. It is not a description limited to human survival, but rather it is a concern with what makes life recognisable in our own terms. It includes those needs that are perceived as essential, as we cannot practically distinguish between needs and the expectations they create. Needs help form expectations which in turn reinforce these needs and embody them with a cultural significance which then overrides the existential.

The nature of this description of a recognisable life can be seen by distinguishing between the common terms, shelter and housing. Housing, in the context of contemporary British culture, involves modern space standards and amenities, security and privacy amongst other issues. It is a place where we can lead a life in accordance with our personally determined requirements subject to the constraints of finance and the law. However, the concept of shelter relates to a basic form of provision of a roof over our head. Shelter thus equates to elementary physical protection. A basic structure would fulfil the basic criteria of shelter, yet not the criteria of the necessity for housing. Housing is thus shelter plus other qualities. These qualities are not universal, but are culturally and personally determined, and thus what constitutes housing is subjective.

The two descriptions of a lack and a necessity, can be further distinguished by their relation to *fulfilment*. When our lack of something has been fulfilled it disappears and we cease to have the lack. It thus ceases to be of concern to us as we now have the particular thing.

By contrast, when a necessity is fulfilled it remains a necessity. We still need housing even when we are currently well housed. This is an important distinction and of particular significance to the identification of an individual to the process of housing. Need as a necessity relates to our libertarian description of solidarity. It describes the little things which make up our world. It is to see them as necessities without which life would not be recognisable. These little things are necessarily personally significant, rather than being universally determined. Yet it is the recognition of what these little things are in the lives of others that create solidarity. This comes through the recognition of what affect the loss of these important little things will have on us, thus implying the significance of the world of others to them. Thus a necessity, and its recognition as such, may be reinforced through our appreciation of the lives of others.

This has implications for the housing process and for the notion of housing need. It is to see the housing process as fulfilling a basic human necessity defined according to what is important in our lives. It is a personalised, qualitative process definable in terms of our personal final vocabulary. The need for housing — it being a basic human necessity — is a condition common to all. What differs is not whether we have a need or not, but rather our ability to fulfil that need and how we go about operationalising that ability. This is particularly so as the commonality of the basic requirement tells us nothing about what housing is and does. It is the fulfilment of that need — how we go about achieving it — that is significant.

In this sense, to be adequately housed is to state that we have fulfilled our need. But that need remains as housing is still as necessary to us. The need does not go away regardless of the current conditions we are residing in. This has important implications for the idea that we can realise a capital gain from housing. If we have to replace one dwelling with another in order to fulfil our need, then any gain may be purely theoretical. It is quite likely that access to the asset may only be possible when our need is extinguished, and, of course, this will mean that others benefit and not us.

The issue is then not strictly one of need itself, but rather one of fulfilment. Housing policy can be seen as a means of fulfilment and I shall show that this fulfilment is a function of an autonomously controlled process. The process is about self description and not a possessive condition that is determined according to external standards and criteria. This description of housing is a non-patterned process, whereby we talk of fulfilment of our own needs and not the determination of what needs are legitimate. This, of course, runs counter to the notion of housing need as it is commonly conceived.

Discourses on housing need tend to concentrate upon the lack of housing and accordingly can be equated to the perceived demand for housing (DOE, 1995a). These discourses may be national attempts to define the lack of "suitable" housing (DOE, 1995a; Whitehead and Kleinman, 1992), or they may be concerned with the assessment of local need (Watson and Harker, 1993, Van Zijl, 1993). Indeed it is a statutory requirement for local authorities to consider the housing needs of its area (Housing Act 1985, S.8).

This lack can be absolute, in the sense of a complete lack of shelter, or it can be seen in terms of a lack of particular space and amenity standards. However, it is frequently an aggregated concept based on population and demographic trends which purports to show any shortfall in potential supply and demand. Whilst these models of need are becoming increasingly sophisticated (e.g., Whitehead and Kleinman, 1992) they still portray the notion of housing need in an unproblematic way. They assume that certain family types have particular requirements which can be identified by government and commentators. The matching of need to fulfilment is seen as simply one of the provision of a certain number of units of a particular type.

The problem with this approach is that the aggregation removes much of the meaning attached to need. By talking of national housing need and demand, these discourses ignore the choices that are implicit within fulfilment. This is particularly significant in that these attempts at meeting need usually refer to social housing aimed at those households unable to provide for themselves through the market. The consequence of this is that housing policy determines the criteria of fulfilment of a particular section of the community. Those able to provide their own housing are less circumscribed and able to be directly involved in the search for a dwelling that fulfils their own expectations.

These needs discourses are essentially top down assessments that seek to determine provision based on centralised criteria. They are based on the premise of governmental competence and legitimacy. The centre makes assumptions about the acceptability of standards and on the affordability of types of provision. It generalises about the nature of needs and consequently diverts the meanings given to housing to its own determination. It is the centre that, through the increasing control of resources, is able to control access to dwellings and, furthermore, through the adjustment of personal and institutional subsidies, to determine their continued use. This has been shown by Page (1993) in his work on the effects of the post 1988 financial regime on housing association provision. The reduction in subsidy has seen a reduction in space standards and the quality of provision. However, the increasing pressure on housing associations as the major providers of public housing has increased the incentive for associations to fill their dwellings to capacity. The result of this is an increasingly "tight fit" between the household and the dwelling. The effect of this centralised policy, which from the centre's perspective presents value for money and the maximisation of limited resources, is to reduce the flexibility within the housing process and to create pressure points that will necessitate some form of remedial action at some point in the future.

Housing need perceived as a necessity would be of a distinctly different character. In this sense we all continue to have a need for housing regardless of our current situation, whether we are currently homeless or under-occupying a large house. This perception of housing is therefore tenure neutral. I do not see housing need as just something which local authorities and housing associations provide, with the financial support and under the direction of central government, for those deemed unable to provide for themselves. Housing need is instead a matter for all tenures and affects them equally.

However, despite its ubiquity, it affects each individual household differently. This is because of the infinite variety of ways in which housing need may be fulfilled. We may be fulfilled with a simple dwelling with few modern amenities that are shared by several households; on the other hand we may consider a dwelling unsatisfactory unless it has a separate room for each member of the household, plus a guest room. This definition of need sees fulfilment as being personally defined and therefore potentially infinitely variable. It follows from this that there can be no external criteria to which we can measure whether our need is currently fulfilled.

In any case our housing need does not disappear merely because it is currently fulfilled. We may not currently lack anything with regard to housing, yet the facility which fulfils us is still needed, or else we cease to be fulfilled. This suggests that the housing process should be as concerned with the maintenance of housing and households as the direct provision of dwellings itself. The housing process should be seen as a support process that permits households to maintain their relation with their dwelling and its surrounding environment. Thus the particular problems with the economic notions of demand and need which underpin the concept of the merit good rely on a concern solely for the provision of goods and services and forget the significance these goods and services may have through their continued use.

A process that perceives housing as a necessity rather than a lack is opaque to central government control. This is because, firstly, government cannot deal with infinite variety, but rather must seek to standardise in order to make processes manageable and understandable, and secondly, the continuity of need means that provision of dwellings to match the number of households achieves nothing of itself. This is precisely why the Modern Conservative's housing policy is proving to be unsustainable. The policy aimed at the expansion of owner occupation could only survive as long as that nature of provision fulfilled the needs of households. In a period of rapidly rising real incomes and house values this was unproblematic. Households were able to concern themselves with their relationships within and beyond the dwelling. Alternatively they could use their current dwelling as an investment in the hope of greater fulfilment in the future. They were not seen as lacking anything, but rather were seen as having an opportunity (Saunders, 1990). However, once this situation altered in the early 1990s, with a significant number of households with negative equity and many unable to sell their current dwelling, the paucity of the approach could be seen. Not only did these households lack the material security they had come to expect from their dwelling, also they were, and perhaps still are, unfulfilled in that their situation is unstable. In effect the nature of their continued housing need has been made transparent by the failure of a centralised housing process.

This description of housing need implies that the process should be under local control, not in the sense of local authorities, housing associations or housing companies, but by the individuals and communities who are to be the users of the resulting provision. If fulfilment is only personally definable the housing process would be at odds with modernist discourse which demands that needs be determined centrally. Such centrality is acceptable because needs are universal and thus capable of central definition. I have suggested that needs are relative and therefore central direction is not competent to determine fulfilment. I therefore need to develop a distinctive discourse of the housing process that recognises the relativity of need and the infinite variety of the means to fulfilment. In order to do so I shall build on this construction of a libertarian community using a different philosophical base to that of modernity.

CHAPTER SIX

A VERNACULAR HOUSING PROCESS

I have shown that modernist discourses on the role of the state are predisposed towards authoritarian direction and centralism. Furthermore I have suggested that the modernist characterisation of the ends of policy misunderstands the variability and incommensurability of human ends and needs. What this implies is that disourses of modernity caricature the complexity of the relation between the dweller, their dwelling and the surrounding environment.One only needs to compare the simplistic linkage between property rights and security posited by Saunders (1990) with the layers of meaning attributed to the home by Gurney (1990). Saunders suggests an absolute meaning attributable to a direct causality, whilst Gurney is content to demonstrate the complexity of deeply personal relations. It is thus too simplistic to attribute the meaning of the home to one particular cause or relation.

Somerville (1993) suggests that the home is "a dynamic unification" (p. 12) of three types of relation. These are spatial relations, suggested by the notion of *privacy*; psychological relations, suggested by *identity*; and social relations, suggested by *familiarity*. Somerville uses these three notions to develop what he terms a "social phenomenology of the home" (p. 12). He does this through a description of the historical, geographical and social construction of privacy, identity and familiarity. According to Somerville, his approach of uniting phenomenological and sociological techniques in the study of home allows him to elucidate the construction of experience and action alongside the creation of social relations. Whilst he admits that this is merely a starting point in the construction of the home as a set of meaningful relations, even the brief description of Somerville's work demonstrates how oversimplistic is the approach taken by modernist discourses with their attempts at total solutions. Both Somerville's and

Gurney's work implies that the personal experience of our housing is of a complexity that leaves it opaque to the generalities of totalising discourses.

Therefore a more nuanced way in which to characterise these relations is needed. This means that the approach of modernist discourse must be rejected and the insights of another philosophical tradition applied instead. Accordingly I shall attempt to relate the work of recent libertarian writers on the built environment, in particular Illich and Turner, with the phenomenology of Heidegger and Norberg-Schulz.

I have suggested that housing is a basic human necessity. It offers physical protection from nature, the elements and the unknown. It provides warmth and offers amenities that allow households to pursue their wider aims. It is possible to suggest that housing has been a necessity in all cultures and throughout the history of human civilisation. Yet to state these simple facts is not to define housing. It does not tell us what housing has been, is now and will be.

What constitutes housing differs over time and across cultures and communities. This difference is determined by the way in which individuals and communities relate to the environment. Thus housing is everywhere different. This is because the lives of households and communities are themselves everywhere different and therefore needs, wants and desires are not uniform and commensurable.

Housing alters with culture because it is not an end in itself. The significance of housing is not in what it is, but what it allows to develop within and through itself. This signification is fundamentally at odds with the property centred ideology of the Modern Conservatives. Instead of concentrating solely on material values, I am concerned with other values. As Birchall has commented with regard to the housing process:

> It's value lies in being a means to other things; physical and emotional security, good health, access to work, to open space, to transport routes, to friends, neighbours and kin. (1988, p. 16)

Any discussion about housing must go further than physical structures and their material value. The discussion must instead focus on housing as a process — as *dwelling*.

The description of dwelling I shall present is the process whereby the individual relates to and with the natural and built environments. It thus means more than the provision and utilisation of housing, as it goes on to consider the meaning that the users give to housing. I shall therefore be concerned to describe how meanings are attributed to housing through this process.

The process of dwelling is a *vernacular* one, in that it arises out of practice and voluntary public discussion. It is thus the opposite of the imposed regime of the Modern Conservatives. This vernacular nature of the process means that outcomes cannot be predetermined outside of the process itself. It is therefore a non-patterned process that arises out of the practice of individuals relating together, emulating each other and showing solidarity through the mutuality of their condition. The starting point for my description is therefore to expound this practice.

6.1. The Role of Traditions

Dwelling can be seen as a process that is not planned, manufactured and imposed on communities and households. It rather develops out of the practice of living as households within communities. This means then that dwelling is more than the production and consumption of houses. It is the interaction of households, individually and collectively, with the environment.

However, this interaction is not a conscious process. We do not relate to the community or the environment necessarily in a deliberative manner. The relationship takes place at the level of "practical consciousness" (Giddens, 1991) where we do not consider or question our actions directly. Practical consciousness is where we use things and are involved in processes in a non-conscious way. It is where we take these things and processes for granted whilst we pursue our more deliberative tasks:

> Most forms of practical consciousness could not be 'held in mind' during the course of social activities, since their tacit or taken-for-granted qualities form the essential condition which allows actors to concentrate on tasks at hand. (Giddens, 1991, p. 36)

Thus we experience the interaction with the environment implicitly whilst we are continuing with our expected activities. The process operates as *equipment* that is *ready-to-hand* in the Heideggerian sense of a tool or implement that becomes an extension of us and thus whose operation is not held in thought (Heidegger, 1962).

We do not consciously dwell because we cannot exist outside of this process — our dwelling encloses us. The ends which dwelling allows for us hides its functioning. As Heidegger states, dwelling:

> ... remains for man's everyday experience that which is from the outset 'habitual'... For this it recedes behind the manifold ways in which dwelling is accomplished. (1993, p. 349-50)

Dwelling is an everyday experience and we live through it. It does not exist as an object separated from our subjectivity.

Dwelling goes beyond the physicality of housing. It is rather a layered process in which our private refuge is linked to public institutions, urban space and human settlement in its general sense (Norberg-Schulz, 1985). It relates the individual and the community through the mutual interdependence of each layer of dwelling. The public level that serves to establish and maintain common values is in part determined by the nature of settlement within the surrounding environment; in part by the exchange of ideas and goods within institutional space, and in part by the value individual households attach to their dwelling which allows them to contribute to the creation and perpetuation of these values.

The implicit nature of dwelling, conceived in this holistic manner, serves to create, and is in turn maintained by, traditions. Dwelling relies on tradition for the transmission of meaning. Yet traditions can be seen as developing out of implicit practices.

The implicit is that which develops non-consciously into the recognisable, the comfortable and the secure. As a result the practice becomes habitual. We repeat and routinise the practice into habit as it reinforces our desire for security and basic trust (Eriksen 1950, 1968; Giddens, 1991). Through interaction at the level of public discussion these habits — our personal final vocabulary — are weaved into traditions that form the cultural support to dwelling.

Dwelling is also about location. It locates the household spatially in a specific dwelling within the environment. It locates the household culturally within a specific community. Furthermore, it locates the household temporally within the traditions of their community in their environment. It is in the social traditions exhibited by dwelling that commonality and cultural identity between households is manifested. This is the reason why access to and control over the dwelling process is seen as central to my description of housing policy.

Traditions are often perceived as being backward looking and restricting. They are seen as representing a less rationalistic age that relied on received wisdom. Indeed, as Gross (1992) has stated, traditions were the explicit targets of modern rationality. Indeed even such writers as Foucault and Heidegger, who at others times emphasise the implicit and the local (e.g., Foucault, 1980; Heidegger, 1993), are suspicious of tradition (Foucault, 1972; Heidegger, 1962). However, traditions should not be seen as conservative and static.

I do not propose a description of dwelling based on the rigidities of existing practices. Rather traditions should be seen as both conserving and dynamic. They preserve those elements of a community and culture that reinforces the values and practices that are meaningful, as frontiers of freedom. These alter over time as the nature of interaction and its context changes. The implicit practices that determine traditions develop and change over time and this will leak into communal activities and values. Traditions may appear to be static because of the implicit nature of their development. The consciousness of tradition is by definition a retrospective action. Moreover, we cannot be conscious of tradition without acknowledging the debt of tradition in the development of that consciousness. As both Derrida (1978) and Gadamer (1975) have suggested in their different ways, we cannot evade the tradition we are part of even as we criticise it.

This, however, means that we can see modernist reflexivity as being not a necessary condition, but merely one result of the process of socialisation. It has been arrived at through social interaction within the restraints of tradition. Modernity cannot therefore be separated from those which preceded and superseded it. Indeed, the periodisation of culture is itself a modernist conceit. Therefore modernity should not be seen as the denial of tradition, but rather as the resignification of a particular tradition into a reified certainty. Modernity thus ignores the dynamic nature of tradition by seeing its rationality and reflexivity as universal and atemporal.

This static position can be countered by the dynamic definition of the postmodern offered by Jencks (1989). He sees the postmodern as a form of "double-coding", which involves an "eclectic mix of any tradition with that of the immediate past (1989, p.7). The postmodern is that which develops the technology and technicality of modernism through its interaction with non-totalising forms of social interaction. Modernity should be seen as just one tradition — the most recent — without being in anyway particularly privileged. Modernity is not therefore the transcendence of traditional forms, but rather is a particular, if somewhat problematical, continuation of it.

There are a number of reasons for this emphasis on tradition. Firstly, to emphasise tradition is to be anti-elitist. It is to refer to how people actually live and thus to talk of tradition is to describe actual practices. A return to tradition in dwelling is to return to recognisability in the dwelling process. Secondly, the traditional process is readily understandable to the users and thus more likely to be inclusive. Thirdly, it is localised through referencing to historical links. Traditions are inimicable to generalised or universal standards. It is where the types of provision are related to a local context. Fourthly, tradition emphasises participation. They are derived from the practices of the users. Fifthly, and perhaps most significantly for our purposes, traditions are important because they show us the means by which needs are fulfilled. It is where individuals, sharing elements of a common vocabulary (Rorty, 1989), have arrived at solutions to questions of need out of the habitual practice of their daily lives. Thus traditions are implicit means of fulfilment. They are expressions of the expectations of individuals mediated through communities in the form of often formalised behaviour and the expression of hopes and beliefs. They offer effective limits (or, to echo Berlin (1969), frontiers) across which an individual will be reluctant to transgress.

Traditions can be seen to express a moral framework of acceptable agency that binds individuals into communities through a tacit recognition of needs, duties and responsibilities. However, these needs, duties and responsibilities are contextualised by their implementation and thus cannot be said to be universalisable. They are forged in a particular set of circumstances and thus they may only be fulfilled in a manner specific to a particular community at a particular time.

Traditions are part of the framework in which the tools of modernity can be controlled and therefore used in a sustainable way. But only in so far as these traditions arise out of communal practices. They cannot be effectively created or recreated by a top down structure. It is only traditions that operate out of a non-patterned, anti-essentialist context that are sustainable and able to reproduce themselves without the reinforcement of a central agency. They are what I shall describe as being *vernacular.*

6.2. Vernacular Dwelling

Traditions of dwelling which emphasise the implicit nature of human practices explicitly reject the notion of "housing-as-property" at the centre of the Modern Conservative description. More generally it stands opposed to the very idea that housing can be ordered through some universal, modernist discourse. However, instead of defining this description as postmodern, and therefore attaching to it the difficulties of a general periodisation, I shall refer to it as *vernacular.* This term now has a particular meaning in architecture, where it is taken to mean structures built without professional architects (Turan, 1990). Whilst there is an obvious connection between this definition and our description of traditional dwelling, I intend to use the term in a broader sense as developed by Illich (1992).

Illich has been generally concerned with the ways in which modernity has taken control away from individuals (1971, 1973, 1992, Illich et Al, 1977, Illich and Sanders, 1988). The modern desire to control and regulate has led to the centralisation and standardisation of daily life. Housing has been transformed into a centrally defined need. In these terms the "housing problem" can be seen as a lack of physical dwelling units, either absolutely or to a particular standard. Housing is thus seen as a product or commodity.

In contrast to the impersonal, centralised, market driven structures of modernism, Illich describes the notion of the vernacular (1992, p. 124). He traces the etymological roots of the word:

> ... vernacular comes from an Indo-germanic root that implies 'rootedness' or 'abode'. It is a latin word used in classical times for whatever was homebred, homespun, home-made — be it slave, a child, food or dress, animal, opinion or a joke. (1992, p. 124)

To say something is vernacular is to say it is self made. It is what comes from the households themselves, rather than something dictated to them from outside. The vernacular is the opposite to that which is *taught*. The vernacular is the habitual, the traditional, the familiar, as opposed to the centrally imposed standard that is taught to us.

Illich states, however, that when the word came into English, it was used in the restricted sense of home-grown, rather than taught, language. Vernacular has come to refer just to untaught, non standard language. Illich now seeks to reinvigorate the word with its classical meaning. This is because he sees the need for a word that:

> ... would designate non-market related activities by which people do things and make do — wants to which, in the process of satisfying them, they also give concrete shape. (1992, p. 124)

He believes that the word vernacular would serve to fulfil this purpose. The use of the word thus goes beyond the notion of non-professional design into a whole set of relations that exist beyond the control of formal relations. Thus the vernacular could be describes as informal relations within the community.

The issue, however, is to extend these relations into dominance over the formal, and thus limit the effects of centralisation and outside control. Thus Illich wishes to "bring into discussion the existence of a vernacular mode of being and doing that extends to all aspects of life" (1992, p. 125). This would be to describe a form of being and doing that is self-generated, self-generating and habitual. The vernacular mode is where locally devised means are developed through practice.

The significance of Illich's definition can be seen when it is related to housing. This view of housing is much wider than the mere physical. Illich accepts that housing is a process based around what it does in the lives of people. Hence his use of the term *dwelling*, to differentiate the authentic and vernacular from the commodified, is significant. It is consistent with our description of human action. Dwelling is about providing the means to undertake a recognisable life. It thus goes beyond the mere provision of shelter and into that of the control that individuals are able to exert over their own condition.

Illich is rightly concerned to develop the political dimension of dwelling. This is where the issue of the vernacular versus the taught is centred, through the political control of resources and the consequent intellectual parameters set by this clash of modes of being and doing. It is fundamentally an issue as to whether our world is self made or made by others. Illich believes that dwelling, as part of the vernacular mode is antagonistic to imposed control. The dwellers themselves determine through practice the characteristics of inhabited space:

> Dwelling is an activity that lies beyond the reach of the architect not only because it is a popular art; not only because it goes on and on in waves that escape his control; not only because it is of tender complexity outside of the horizon of mere biologists and systems analysts; but above all because no two communities dwell alike. Habit and habitat are almost the same. (1992, p. 56)

Sustainable dwelling is beyond prescription by professionals or academics. This is because it can only be made by those experiencing and making it as an habitual and self made process. Dwelling forms a total environment — a lifeworld — developed through habit and practice: "It is an art that can only be picked up" (1992, p. 56). It is not learned or imposed, but rather it is what we do as part of a community. Indeed it is part of our integration into the community:

> Each person becomes a vernacular builder and a vernacular speaker by growing up and moving from one initiation to the next...(1992, p. 56)

Dwelling is that which is created out of the lives of people — it is how we live. Illich is thus describing a layered process of dwelling similar to that encountered in the work of Norberg-Schulz (1985).

According to Norberg-Schulz dwelling refers to spaces and places, both in terms of how they are used and what this use means to the individual and the community. Dwelling is accorded with three meanings. Firstly, it means to meet others for the exchange of products, ideas and feelings, where we experience life as a multitude of possibilities. This, of course, relates to our concept of a community based upon public discussion. Secondly, dwelling means to accept a set of common values. It is to achieve and live with the results of those encounters and accept the limits they emplace upon us. Thirdly, it means to be ourselves, where we have a small, chosen world of our own. It is where the important things from which our private world are created are protected and nurtured. Of course, these three meanings are interrelated. We are able to be ourselves through the security of a common bond within a community of individuals able to meet freely and exchange. Norberg-Schulz recognises this when he states that "when dwelling is accomplished our wish for belonging and participation is fulfilled" (1985, p. 7).

Sustainable dwelling allows us to both identify with our total environment and to orient ourselves with a focus — our private dwelling — and with known axes and pathways in the environment (Norberg-Schulz, 1985). The process of dwelling can thus be seen as that which enhances and maintains our familiarity with our environment as a natural, social, cultural and political entity.

The greatest threat to this inclusive nature of dwelling is, what Illich terms, the world of the modern resident. The resident "lives in a world that has been made" (1992, p. 57). This is a world that is centrally controlled, where housing is provided for people. Dwelling, as a process of engagement with our surroundings, is denied to us. Illich depicts humans, as residents, as being packed into "garages". This is a deliberate connotation with parking or the storing away of objects. These objects are put away for the night, protected from the elements and from any violation, but where there is no agency to determine the nature of this habitation. It is where the residents have become equipment themselves rather than being dwellers using equipment within the process of dwelling. Residents become equipment in the process of political control:

> Housing provides cubicles in which residents are housed. Such housing is planned, built and equipped for them. To be allowed to dwell minimally in one's own housing constitutes a special privilege: only the rich may move a door or drive a nail in a wall. The vernacular space of dwelling is replaced by the homogenous space of the garage. Settlements look the same from Taiwan to Ohio and from Lima to Peking. Everywhere you find the same garage for the human — shelves to store the workforce overnight, handy for the means of its transportation. Inhabitants dwelling in spaces they fashion have been replaced by residents sheltered in buildings produced for them duly registered as consumers of housing, protected by the Tenant's or Credit Receivers Act (1992, p. 57-8)

Several significant points can be pulled from this description. Firstly, housing is provided for people, rather than by them. It is made and equipped by others, according to standards made by others. Secondly, housing has become homogenised by this form of centralised provision. As a result it has lost its cultural significance. The vernacular has given way to a uniform, culturally anonymous form of provision. Thirdly, this provision is provided to facilitate production and consumption. It is organised to meet the needs of a market economy which is now global in its interests and its effects. Thus there is a uniformity across cultures that ignores the ability of individuals, within local communities, to create their own dwelling through interaction with their environment. This has been demonstrated not only in the work of Jacobs (1961) as occurring in USA and Power (1987) in Britain, but is also a phenomena in Nigeria (Uduku, 1994) which has seen a transformation of traditional styles and a use of globalised technologies. Uduku links this process of transforming traditional dwellers into "residents" as a result of dominance of "Western global production models" (p. 668) and the increasing adoption of free market principles by Third World governments such as in Nigeria. The result is a creeping uniformity of provision as the same totalising housing policies follow the adoption of these equally totalising economic policies. Turner (1976) has shown this process of homogenisation occurring also in Latin America.

Illich believes that two modes can oppose, what he terms, modern society's "ban on spatial self-assertion" (1992, p. 58). These are the non-modernised and the postmodern. The non-modernised, characteristically in the Third World, are still able to pursue vernacular dwelling as the mechanisms of central control are not in place. By postmodern Illich is referring to squatting movements and attempts to repopulate the semi-desolate areas of major cities. According to Illich, these informal community based structures find it possible to facilitate the vernacular because of the inability of central authority to maintain sufficient control. Uduku (1994) shows that this is indeed the case in Nigeria, where there is a growing informal sector using traditional forms of materials and techniques amenable to small scale construction. However, this sector has not simply returned to the old forms of provision and dwelling types. It has rather approached the dilemma of inadequate dwelling through a mix of modern dwelling types and traditional methods of construction and development. It is therefore perhaps difficult to suggest whether Uduku's example is of the premodern or the postmodern. This is, however, a problem of Illich's clear cut distinction between the pre- and postmodern rather than with the thesis that the informal sector can continue with strategies of self assertion outside of the determination of modernity.

Therefore a contrast can be made between the commodification that Illich sees as typifying modernity and the existential values of the vernacular. Modernity's purpose has been to turn dwelling from the home-made into a mass produced economic unit. Housing has therefore become a scarce resource rationed through a market as opposed to a free relation with the local environment.

Dwelling can be characterised as a concern for human, rather than for material, values. My description has suggested that there is a fundamental division between these two value systems. Moreover it is our belief that a concern for material standards and values inhibits dweller control.

As Turner (1972, 1976) has indicated, the problem with the application of standards is that they are often "ought" statements. These standards are what dwellers ought to have according to professionals and experts. These uniform, centrally imposed standards are often counterproductive. This is because of two reasons:

> Firstly, where there is a significant gap between the levels of investment they require and the effective demand; and secondly, when that gap cannot be closed with subsidies, whether through lack of financial resources or lack of will on the government's part. (1972, p. 150)

The problem of a discourse of standards is that it couches the issue of housing in purely quantitative terms. It is where policy is reduced to more being always better than less. It is where housing is seen as a *noun*. Turner states that such an analysis fails "to distinguish between what things are, rationally speaking, and what they do in peoples' lives" (1972, p. 152).

Turner articulates two case studies carried out in Mexico City in 1971. He compares the provisional shack of a rag-picker and his family with that of a modern government subsidised dwelling lived in by a semi-employed mason and his family.

The dwelling of the rag-picker and his family is near to their source of income, close to family and friends, and cheap enough to allow them to survive with the hope of obtaining a better dwelling as their prospects improve. It thus offers them considerable freedom and Turner thus refers to it as the "supportive shack" (1976, p. 54). It is very basic accommodation, yet it fulfils the family's immediate needs and allows them to control their environment.

However, the modern house of the mason's family is located away from their network of friends and, crucially, away from the mason's place of employment. The mason pays out five percent of his income in transport costs to and from work, in addition to the fifty five percent spent on rent and utility charges. Moreover, his wife had previously run a small vending business from their previous dwelling, which was now forbidden under the tenancy regulations. Thus their income has been reduced as their housing and transport costs have risen. Turner refers to this case as the "oppressive house" (1976, p. 56). Thus an improvement in material standards can be counterproductive because, being based on abstract standards, they cannot take into account particular needs and conditions. Turner thus concludes from these cases that material standards are not necessarily the most useful measure:

> Some of the poorest dwellings, materially speaking, were clearly the best, socially speaking, and some, but not all of the highest standard dwellings, were the most socially aggressive. (1976, p. 52)

This implies that the usefulness of housing for the users is independently variable from material standards and it therefore follows that conventional standards — based on material values and national determinations of need — are unlikely to succeed in their purpose:

> Quantitative methods cannot describe the relationship between things, people and nature — which is just where experience and human values lie. (1976, p. 62)

Housing, as I have already stated, is not an end in itself, but is rather a process of relationships with our immediate environment. It is what helps to give meaning to our world.

To follow Turner, it is the relationships between people, nature and things — between the dweller, the immediate environment and the dwelling — that are crucial. These relations indicate the importance of control. What is important is the determination of the relationships between people, nature and things, and whether there is any form of mediation between the dweller, the environment and the dwelling. It is about how we put ourselves in comfort with nature. It is thus to construct a sustainable process where our dwelling is embedded in the environment and not separated from it. How these relationships are controlled is the most significant issue in attaining sustainability and this overides the material. Thus a distinction should be made between an object and its meaning as is shown by Turner's descriptions of the supportive shack and the oppressive house.

Of course, the role of material value cannot be ignored entirely, yet this is only one part in a complex interrelationship that gives the product its meaning. It is what we can do with the dwelling — its functions in use and our perception of them — that is crucial. This, of course, concerns issues of affordability and material value, but not to the extent that these characteristics override all others. Affordability relies on use, rather than determining it:

> ... if housing is perceived as functions of what housing does in the lives of its users — of the roles which the process plays in their life history — and not in the material qualities of the physical products, then the material worth of the products and the manner of their production are entirely dependent on their highly variable uses. Their uses, in turn, vary along with the changing demands imposed by changes in the context, or in the location of the process in the same context. (1972, p. 159)

This leads Turner to state that "(i)n the final analysis who can evaluate them" (1972, p. 153).

If use overrides material standards, and if this use is highly variable according to the dwellers and their particular context, then only the users are in a position to decide whether a product fulfils their needs. These uses obviously relate to the values that people place on their activities and the different parts of their lives. Housing can thus assist or hinder these priorities and this is why housing should be seen as a process that "acts as a vehicle for personal fulfilment" (1972, p. 153).

Furthermore housing is "an existentially significant activity" (Turner, 1972, p. 153) in that the ends of life depend upon it. It is therefore an activity particularly amenable to both personal direction and direct participation. The distinction between the existentially significant and insignificant is important in understanding housing. It is to make the distinction between housing as a noun and as a verb. Treating housing as a noun is to see it as an end in itself with its own value. It is where housing is a product, and where policy is about the provision of a given number of products for consumption.

However, on the other hand:

> ... if housing is treated as a verbal entity, as a means to human ends, as an activity rather than as a manufactured and packaged product, decision-making power of necessity remains in the hands of the users themselves. (Turner, 1972, p. 154)

To accept that housing is an existentially significant activity is thus to see the need to make our world ourselves, rather than having it produced for us.

If housing's value is in what it does — in how it is and can be used — then this value is dependent on the user. Thus the use overrides the product itself. The product can be significant, or given meaning, only through the values applied to it by the user and therefore it should be self-determined. Thus by placing human values to the fore in the dwelling process the necessary controllers are seen to be the dwellers themselves. However, I would go further and suggest that sustainable dwelling can only exist when it is personalised and self-directed rather than being directed externally.

Turner identifies those non-quantifiable roles which the housing process can play in the lives of individuals, and thus why it is an existentially significant activity. These roles are to provide identity, security and opportunity for the dweller. It is the operationalisation of these roles that differentiates the discourse of dwelling from that of property rights. Vernacular dwelling offers identity, security and opportunity. It gives meaning by relating dwellers to the things themselves. It is the lifeworld of identification with implicitly understood things — it demonstrates the practical consciousness of the secure dweller. The control of this world — control that comes from a secure identity — offers opportunity. The control of dwelling allows choice in relationships because no individual or agency necessarily mediates between us and our purposes. This shows where the process of vernacular dwelling is linked to the description of the individual I have presented. This linkage is found in the ability of individuals to self create.

6.3. Self Creation

The process I have outlined should be seen as a means, but not to any particular end. The ends of those who would seek to benefit from the process are many and varied. They cannot be stated in a categorical sense. This is because there is no underlying unifying principle to which I can make recourse. The process is thus one which will allow the personally defined ends to be satisfied, free from interference.

The process is therefore necessarily vague. I have not described the mechanics of a system of provision, but rather only the parameters in which any mechanism can be governed. Some mechanisms will be too unwieldy and insensitive to operate within these limits — they will lack the sufficient flexibility. Other mechanisms may lack the robust flexibility necessary to cope with a multiplicity of uses. I shall offer some comments about how a policy framework may appear in Part Three, but this will only be a very basic outline that deals with the possible implications of a process under user control. Such a process is necessarily unpredictable. This is, of course, a challenge but also its most enticing feature — it mirrors the unpredictability of a social life free of the patterning of centralising discourses.

My immediate concern, however, is to describe how this particular process offers the best prospect of equalising opportunities to self creation. I thus have to show how the process I have discussed links with the description of the individual I have also presented.

I have described a process that seeks merely to equalise the opportunities for self creation and then allow individuals the freedom to exploit or neglect their opportunities. It does not seek to dictate, define or to intervene to "create" citizens in its own image. It is rather based on a description of autonomy as the freedom of personal agency. It is where we are free from manipulation by others. We are not circumscribed or defined by others, but rather we are free to describe ourselves in our own terms.

Furthermore it is to recognise that moral agency is located at the level of the individual. Moral legitimacy is embodied in individuals and radiates out from them in their relations with others in the community. Legitimacy is not seen as being located in the state or the community. It is rather located in individuals voluntarily coming together as a community of free participants. Morality is acquired not through rationality and the search for the "true essence of humanity", but rather through individuals having freedom against the imposition of "truth".

Of course, I am not proposing an unlimited role for the individual. It is not realistic to suggest that individuals are totally free, unrestrained agents. Individuals cannot fail to engage in social life and be involved in communal activities. Dwelling is a layered and interdependent process (Norberg-Schulz, 1985). However, my description of moral legitimacy at the level of the individual can be sustained by an emphasis on the nature of this involvement. The communities I have described are those that develop out of free dialogue. They are therefore voluntary associations which develop from the bottom upwards. Any circumscription is self-imposed and based on the agreed outcomes of free dialogue. Our vision is therefore one of autonomy voluntarily surrendered when it is seen as rational to do so, but not forcibly removed in the name of some formula of universal rationality.

The notion of a voluntary relation within a community can be developed through a description of what I mean by the notion of self creation. Self creation can be defined as the *ability to define ourselves*. Thus autonomy is where we are able to self create — or define — our moral agency and connect it spatially and temporally within a community. We are autonomous because we have security in our being, given by this commonality, and therefore we are able to radiate outwards towards the community through the boundary of our private dwelling. Self creation is where this boundary is one we have defined and formed ourselves. This description of autonomy as self creation can be related to Heidegger's concept of *authenticity* .

According to Heideggerian phenomenology, to be authentic is to accept our condition as individuals thrown into an otherwise incomprehensible world where the only certainty is our mortality. Instead of accepting prevailing attitudes and conventions because of our anxiety over our eventual death, we are determined to take responsibility for our *being-in-the-world* (Heidegger, 1962). This can be re-described to suggest it is where we recognise our individuality as a set of potentialities. It is where we have opportunities for self creation:

> ... while in authentic mode, we maintain an independence of thought and action, and subsequently feel 'in charge' of the way our life is experienced. (Spinelli, 1989, p. 109)

It is where we give meaning to things by understanding them in the intimacy of their use, as equipment ready-to-hand. Moreover, in the authentic mode we recognise and accept change and difference:

> ... our experiences of ourselves and others (are) characterised by openness, flexibility, co-operation and responsibility. (Spinelli, 1989, p. 110)

Furthermore "our authentic stance acknowledges both an equality of importance and a status between self and others" (Spinelli, 1989, p. 110). We recognise others and their ideas and initiatives as being equal to us. We are thus open to other final vocabularies than our own.

It is important to realise that Heidegger's division between the authentic and the inauthentic is one that exists within individuals rather than between them. There are not two distinct types of people, but rather we are capable of being both at different times.

This description of authenticity allows us to develop dwelling as a condition of our humanity — as part of our being-in-the-world. When we dwell authentically we are aware of our individuality and exercise it positively. Thus we can say that dwelling is something which we all do, yet when we experience it authentically we dwell in a matter that is everywhere different, because authenticity is where we act autonomously.

Authenticity is where we recognise our own individuality and accept responsibility for our predicament. It is where the individual rejects the externally imposed — "the taught" (Illich, 1992) — in preference for our own purposes. We radiate outwards from the boundary of the self on our own terms and accept responsibility for the relations corresponding to this radiation. It is not then a form of atomism, but rather *self description*. We are defined from the inside.

We act authentically when we do not simply conform to some notion of human nature or essence predicated by a metaphysical foundation. We recognise the self as a set of potentialities to be exploited, rather than being a set of receptors to cultural norms. This is not to reject cultural norms, but to suggest that they are not a sufficient prerequisite for satisfactory relationships in a community. Solidarity should be seen as deriving from a recognition of our own individuality. If we see ourselves as a set of potentialities then we must perceive these qualities in others. Authenticity leads us to a perceived equality between ourselves and others. We should respect the vocabularies of others in as much as we respect our own.

Authenticity is linked to autonomy in that they are both related to personal agency. Autonomy is the legitimate exercise of personal agency. Authenticity is the recognition and understanding of the significance of this legitimacy. The authentic mode is thus expressed in autonomous action. Therefore both autonomy and authenticity are integral to the expression of personal identity. This identity has been described as being protected by the housing process under local control, and thus where we can dictate use. It is a process where we are able to construct a relational web around our ontological and emotional needs and through which we can develop our public selves. We are thus orientated by our dwelling through its provision of both a centre and as the opening up of pathways into the world (Norberg-Schulz, 1985).

Housing is not experienced as property, but rather as a web of personal relations. Its meaning is derived from the manner in which it is used and through what we are able to achieve because of it. Housing therefore has no intrinsic value of itself, it being a vessel for other intrinsically valuable relations. Therefore the significance of housing can be restated as being the personal means to fulfilment of those things authentically defined by an autonomous individual.

Housing can be seen as equipment (Heidegger, 1962). It is *ready-to-hand* when its functions fulfil the need for security, intimacy and identity. The achievement of these ends are implicit because we are too busy using it as the means to fulfil our ends. Its use is regular and complementary and thus we see it as habitual. The use of housing as a means for fulfilment is not then consciously acknowledged unless a problem develops with the equipment so that it becomes *unready-to-hand*. When a problem arises the equipment becomes *present-to-hand*. This is where it is consciously perceived as a thing in itself rather than as a means. This may help us to understand why a minor maintenance problem in our dwelling often creates a level of anxiety disproportionate to the seriousness of the defect. The problem brings the nature of the dwelling into consciousness allowing the complexity of the relationships and dependencies within dwelling to be seen. A defect breaks the habitual nature of dwelling and shows its ontological, emotional and material significance. The loss of our dwelling shows even more graphically its significance to us by destroying the implicit sense of orientation and identification given us by the boundary that housing provides. Again it is when the process is in crisis or is not functioning — where it is equipment present-to-hand — that its significance is made most apparent.

As I have shown the habitual and the implicit connects with the significance of tradition in vernacular dwelling. The implicit is that which develops non-consciously into the recognisable, the comfortable, the reinforcing and the secure. As a result of these features the implicit becomes habitual. The process of interaction leads to the weaving of these individual habits into traditions that form the cultural support to dwelling.

Thus the significance of self creation is that it relates solidarity with tradition and thus to the implicit level in the lives of individuals. Solidarity is seen to derive out of the bonds of tradition and shared history that have in turn developed from the habitual daily act of living. Thus the authentic self creation of autonomous individuals leads to traditions through dialogue within a framework of implicit acts. In this sense, solidarity relies on the vernacular processes of authentic dwelling.

I have suggested that one of the primary effects of modernist forms of provision is to universalise culture and therefore to universalise concepts of need. Culture has to an extent been globalised. This results in the imposition and explicit acceptance of a universal epistemic of technical problem solving based upon the existing centres of global dominance. Thus local conditions are stated in terms of solving technical problems, and solutions are framed by means dictated by the industrialised nations. In this way traditions are ignored or counteracted, often deliberately as they are seen to represent the primitive and the premodern (Illich, 1992). Needs are no longer expressed in vernacular terms, but in response to this modernist agenda of problem definition and solving. The problem of this situation is that the unsustainability we have described with regard to the Modern Conservatives is itself universalised as writers such as Turner (1972; 1976), Skinner and Roddell (1983) and Mathey (1992) have shown. Turner in particular has shown how mass public provision built to Western standards of amenity are unsustainable in the developing world, resulting in a revitalisation of vernacular dwelling processes in order to circumvent and mitigate the failures of these modernist standards. Thus Turner depicts the illegal squatter settlements around many Latin American cities as the re-emergence of the vernacular rather than as a problem to be solved. These settlements are examples of the diverse and fragmentary responses to needs that have characterised the idea of the postmodern. It is where the fulfilment of need is recontextualised by action directly by and for the local community.

Central to the dichotomy between modernism and a re-emerging vernacular is that of the control of the environment. Universal prescription implies a centralisation of power in order to impose uniformity. The squatter settlements in the developing world are examples of where centralised power does not extend sufficiently to impose a uniform prescription. In this sense local centres of power develop around the distribution of land and the provision of services. In addition informal forms of mutual aid develop into more formal traditions of operation within these communities. Both the social structure and the built form of these communities combine traditional forms and modern resourcing and materials thus creating a postmodern environment essentially under local control (for example see Ramirez et al, 1992). This is a form of self creation developing into vernacular processes.

These principles of user control and decentralised power to create a vernacular environment are relevant to the so called developed world. Control over housing is just as central to fulfilment of needs in Britain as in the developing world. What differs is the context in which issues of control are placed. Whilst this context is indeed different the essential issues that flow out of it are basically similar. Local control relates to choice, firstly in terms of the opportunities for self creation and the ability to affect the context itself, and secondly, the access to resources that translates choice into empowerment. These two issues can be brought together in the concept of *effective choice*. This notion relates to the practical possibility of fulfilment. It does not describe choice in the abstract as a general right as both Hayek and Nozick do, but rather it relates to specific conditions of empowerment — *to choices between alternatives.*

The amount of control over ourselves and the environment around us directly relate to the level of effective choice that we enjoy. Effective choice is thus where opportunities for self creation are translated into action. It is where the autonomous individual acts, or is able to act, in an authentic manner. I shall now explore how this ability may be operationalised through a policy framework.

PART THREE

THE LIMITS OF

HOUSING POLICY

CHAPTER SEVEN

A FRAMEWORK FOR POLICY

Any policy developed as an alternative to the modernist form of provision must attempt to operate outside of the particular epistemological framework I have described in Part One. I must therefore avoid any attempt at devising a universally applicable pattern for dwelling. Instead I should aim for a more modest description of a framework for policy that will offer the possibility for user control and self description. Such a policy framework cannot be described with any precision, but merely as an outline of those principles which will allow self directed policies to develop within the local context that individuals and communities find themselves. It is a policy framework concerned with providing the means to fulfilment, rather than seeing a particular end in terms of aggregates and standards. Such a framework would not prescribe a form or type of dwelling. It would rather be a policy, to reiterate Rorty's words, that would seek to "equalise opportunities for self-creation and then leave people alone to use, or neglect their opportunities" (1989, p. 85).

Such a framework offers opportunities for the development and possible fulfilment of potentialities. This implies a level of control over the means to fulfilment and the access to resources to ensure that self determined ends are attainable. We are then to be left to use or neglect opportunities that we have created. Thus we are not informed of what our opportunities are to be, nor are they externally circumscribed (except insofar as they impinge on the opportunities of others). The idea of personal agency implies that any policy framework must have limits placed upon it. There must not be opportunities for power or resources to be appropriated or concentrated. Thus the policy should be concerned with the imposition of limits on external agency and interference. The central facets of a sustainable housing policy aimed at enhancing effective choice will thus be concerned with *limits, control and access*. However, these can only be stated as principles, as the details of any policy will necessarily depend upon the particular context. The role of policy makers is thus merely to ensure that a framework is in place and then allow a particular set of relations to develop.

The primary prerequisite for this framework is the imposition of limits on the activities and actions of government. In any community government is the organisation with the resources and strategic capacity to direct these resources. Therefore government has a significant role to play in any policy framework. However, as Turner (1976) has stated, we need to distinguish between the users and the regulators in any system; in this case between the dwellers and government. Government may initially control resources and be able to regulate distribution, but it is not able to control use in a sustainable manner. Thus, in recognition of this, one of the primary roles of government should be set limits for action. These limits should restrict involvement in the dwelling process to the provision of resources and a framework of administrative law. These laws would also set limits to private action that may restrict the ability of others to use or neglect their opportunities for self creation. Such a body of law would proscribe what it is not possible to do. It would place a boundary around processes and action. However, within those boundaries individuals and agencies may operate as they see fit.

Thus government could lay down certain standards which would protect the well being of others and the environment; it could prohibit the use of certain dangerous materials and techniques in the development process; it could prohibit development in certain areas to protect natural habitats and green belts; and so on. But it would not determine what is built, or how it is built, or by whom within these broad limits. This is to differentiate, as Turner (1976) does, between limits to action and lines of action. The former creates possibility and opportunity, the latter offers only one possible option. Moreover it is essential that these limits be sanctioned by the lowest possible level of government, thus ensuring that any restrictions arise out of public dialogue and not centralised dictat.

The role of government is not therefore that of a policy maker itself, but rather as a guarantor of the framework in which individuals relate together to create de facto policy through effective legitimate action. This, of course means that the government must retain some form of sanction to enforce these limits. It is important here, however, that the power of sanction is itself limited to the administrative level and that it be operated at the local level. Government should be localised so that it is controlled by communities small enough to allow for effective dialogue. This implies a fundamental re-ordering of the nature of government away from the centralising notions of modernity and towards a radically decentralised administration controllable by the locality. This may mean a considerable reduction in the functions of government, but if this is so, it will have been arrived at out of the very process of public discussion that it is at the heart of this libertarian framework.

A means of ensuring that limits are maintained is through making layers of government dependent on the level below it for its powers and finance. Thus the basic community or parish level would determine the role of the district which in turn would determine the role of the region and so on. The easily foreseeable problems of achieving agreement across diverse and incommensurable communities is to be seen as a virtue of this system as it is the best hope that power will not become concentrated at one level or in one place.

Limits on the action of government are essential if the prerequisite of control at the lowest level of competence is to be achieved. If individuals are to be able to pursue their own ends through the dwelling process, they must themselves control the means. This implies that whilst the various layers of government will provide both a framework of law and the necessary resources it should then abdicate the control of these resources to the users. All that is required of government is this and nothing more. It has no reason to set detailed standards or building regulations and it need only decide upon aggregates in response to the demands placed upon it by the users coming together to decide on quantity and distribution.

Such a framework will necessitate the ultimate responsibility for action being located at the lowest level where there are no superior agents to the users themselves. This implies that there is an effective limit on the size of local government. I would suggest that the lowest — and most influential level — should be small enough to allow for direct individual intervention. This limitation on size is necessary to maintain the integrity of existentially significant activities and therefore ensure that power is itself limited to the parameters of the direct participants.

Control at the level of the users does not imply that there is no role for housing and other professionals. However, this role will be radically different from that experienced at present. Some dwellers may wish to build their own dwelling, and a majority will purchase their dwelling from amongst the existing stock and therefore will not need conventionally defined housing management services. However, I have described housing as a means to fulfilment — as equipment ready-to-hand — which is not transparent to consciousness. Housing may therefore not be the explicit, conscious centre of all our lives. A significant proportion, indeed probably a majority, will not wish to self-build, nor will they wish to manage their own property and the surrounding environment directly in the sense that local housing management is generally conceived. The priority (and this is the case regardless of tenure) may rather be to ensure the existential fastness of our dwelling. Therefore the form of management that we will seek to engage in is the control of the boundary that private dwelling offers for identification and orientation. Participation in communities is dependent upon this security. This may account for the relative apathy towards tenant participation initiatives. These initiatives tend to emphasise issues relating to the public or external environment and are thus of less immediate interest to the majority of dwellers. It is only when the external environment threatens the viability of relations within private space that participation is guaranteed and often effective. However, once the threat recedes mass participation will again decline into apathy. This reiterates the important message of my description of the vernacular, that it is for dwellers to determine the agenda of significance.

Effective user control is that which is individuated. In this way users are able to voluntarily orientate themselves with others who are equally secure in this environment. Individual control allows participation to be positive rather than a reaction to an external threat. Of course, it is perfectly possible, indeed most likely, that many dwellers will delegate the management of the process to others. What is important therefore is not the day-to-day control of the process, but rather the ability to determine both how that process is to managed and what input we wish to make.

Control is currently differentiated according to tenure. Owner occupiers experience greater control over their dwelling than tenants and have greater choice in determining the location and type of dwelling within the constraints of disposable income. The role of government as a regulator should therefore be to equalise the possibility for control. However, this should be done by increasing the control experienced by tenants rather than limiting that enjoyed by owner occupiers. This could be achieved by guaranteeing participative structures whereby tenants are able to direct their landlord.

Housing management must be directed by the dwellers if they are to have effective choice. This facet of control is crucial as the vast majority of dwellings are already existing and therefore would not have been built under the direction of the potential users. Control over management and maintenance of the existing stock will accordingly be of much greater significance than control over building.

This point has been recognised by Bhatti (1993) in his use of the concept of "prosumers", described as "people who consume the goods and services they produce" (p. 104). Bhatti believes that the distinction between producers and consumers in housing is becoming increasingly ambiguous. Households as prosumers are those who define their own housing needs and the relationship to those providing these services. In response to this development the role of housing professional is to "provide technical aid and facilitate, but (they) do not actually control the process" (1993, p. 105). Professionals are thus facilitators who allow and enhance the users' effective choice in the dwelling process.

Bhatti realises that to achieve this position professionals and the organisations they represent need to give up their ability to control the housing process. Hence the framework I am outlining suggests an intellectual shift as much as a structural change. It needs housing professionals to understand their role as a subordinate one determined by their erstwhile clients and customers. In a sense it requires housing professionals (and others such as academics and commentators who depend on housing for their livelihoods), the majority of whom are owner occupiers, to generalise the freedoms and controls which they enjoy over their dwellings to those whose dwellings they control. Housing professionals routinely intervene in the affairs of tenants in ways that they would find intolerable themselves.

The framework would not include housing organisations in their current form, and this too will have considerable implications for professional practice. Organisations would be dispersed into small local units in which direct participation within the structures is possible. As Turner's studies in Mexico have shown the notion of economies of scale in housing is one that ignores the necessary referencing of the dwelling to the user (Turner, 1976). Scale in dwelling is therefore an individuated notion, or rather the concept of economies of scale is only valid if the point of reference is the efficiency of the organisation and not the user's perception of the service provided.

The remit given to the players within these localised structures would be determined by the users themselves. There are grounds for doubting whether current housing management practice is indeed necessary in the localised framework I am describing. This is not to contradict my earlier point regarding the implicit nature of dwelling and the consequent lack of direct involvement, but rather to call into question the need for the invasive methods used at present.

Current housing management techniques can be said to be based on a form of *tenure apartheid*, whereby certain households are deemed to lack competence because of their tenure. British households living in local authority and housing association dwellings seemingly need to be managed by professionals. This means that the property is maintained to the organisations standards (which are in turn directly influenced by statute) and any problems deemed significant by the organisation are attended to. In return the behaviour of these households are circumscribed by rules concerning the use of the dwelling. Landlords are even able to impose standards of behaviour, in particular with regard to non-domestic use of the dwelling and relations with other tenants, that do not relate to the conduct of the tenancy. Thus a tenant who fulfils all of the landlord's requirements regarding rent payments and the upkeep of the property may still be evicted because they are deemed to be harassing a neighbour. This, of course, is not to suggest that harassment is a legitimate form of behaviour, but rather that the landlord's sanction is inappropriate. It would be akin to leaving it up gunsmiths to ban murderers from owning a gun rather than the community punishing them for taking the life of another (and is indeed similar to the practice of banning the driver who ran over a child rather than punishing him for the irresponsible use of a potentially dangerous machine). It is a form of sanction that puts the rights over property above human relations.

However, when these tenants exercise their right to buy their property these restrictions are removed. Through the act of acquiring a mortgage and becoming an owner occupier the household is now deemed competent in the management and maintenance of their housing. Moreover, any issue of harassment becomes a matter not for a housing professional, but for the police and the courts — it is no longer seen as a housing management issue. Owner occupiers are deemed to be responsible citizens capable of exercising choices and in no need of direction regarding the upkeep of their dwelling. Tenants however, are assumed to be the opposite and may only prove otherwise by leaving the tenure. However, in reality there is no reason to suggest that tenants are incapable of determining their own needs and exercising choices in the same way as owners. It would be a difficult position to maintain that one becomes more capable merely because one has acquired a mortgage.

The issue of access to resources is equally important. Indeed it is access that activates control. If individuals are to fulfil their housing needs they must have access to an adequate level of resources. However, as with use, adequacy can only be determined at the level of the users themselves. It is unlikely that centralised standards of provision will achieve this as they are driven by notions of economic efficiency and value for money rather than self creation. This therefore necessitates the location of resources at the lowest level. Housing finance and resources should be available through local institutions, which are guaranteed but not controlled by government. These locally controlled agencies would maximise appropriate housing within a local context, and this means that the level and type of support should be determined locally. This will ensure that a variety of provision is available, and to a variety of players, be they individuals, co-operatives or other agents acting on behalf of individuals and groups. Local control would ensure the minimum of prescription.

Assistance could be given to those with no or low incomes through means tested benefits or vouchers providing services in kind. This support scheme would replace all other forms of housing subsidy. Thus each tenure would be equal with the financial advantages and tax exemptions of owner occupation being withdrawn. This would also serve to stabilise the volatile owner occupied market and to decommodify it by reducing the possibility for wealth creation through property ownership.

The notion of means testing is a controversial one. It has long been one of the shibboleths of the mainstream left that benefits should be universally available. It is felt that means testing attaches a stigma to the recipient which makes them vulnerable and may mean that some individuals are reluctant to apply for them. Furthermore, it is argued that some people will be unaware of their entitlement and thus not claim them.

I can quickly dispense with these objections. Firstly, the notion of universal benefits is predicated on the premise that there are universal needs — as we have the same needs they should be met in the same way. I have already shown the deficiency of these arguments and suggested that needs are relative. If this is the case then there is no reason to suggest that needs should not be dependent on the particular circumstances of the individuals themselves. Secondly, the lack of knowledge that some people may have about their entitlements may be due to the complexity of a nationally administered system. If a system were administered locally according to locally determined rules then one could expect it to be more understandable.

Whilst I cannot suggest how these locally determined systems would operate in minute detail, I can propose that any form of assistance should seek to give individuals the maximum opportunity to choose the most appropriate form of dwelling, either individually or collectively. Resources would then become owned either individually or collectively, thus allowing permanent access into the housing system and assisting the creation of flexible housing careers. Such a system would not remove the freedom an individual may have to seek housing finance elsewhere, nor would it prevent those wishing to opt out altogether from doing so.

Thus a framework for policy consistent with effective choice centres on limits, control and access. I have shown that these three factors interlink together. However, out of necessity I have only provided the most general of outlines, as to do otherwise would be to contradict the descriptions on which this framework is based. The framework seeks to allow for diversity, flexibility and self creation amongst communities of individuals whose needs are not necessarily commensurable. The framework is intended to allow individuals, working alone or through co-operation, to determine and control those means that best fulfil their ends. The policy framework should not aim to fulfil any particular purpose, but rather to facilitate the determination of self determined purposes — it should be a framework that allows the users to make policy by their actions.

Of course, I cannot guarantee that this framework will not develop over time into something unintended. I have no reason to claim its stability in perpetuity. The danger of self directed action is its unpredictability, and this is exactly its virtue. This framework, like any system I can imagine can offer only stability now. It cannot offer it into the future. All that I am credibly able to do then is to describe a framework that allows for the contingency of possibility. It should therefore be localised and minimal, yet able to offer empowerment. Such a task is a difficult one, and it may need constantly reforging in the light of current practices and choices. However, it is only such a loose framework that recognises what housing does — as a means towards meeting our own ends free from interference.

CONCLUSION

The purpose of this essay has been to offer a critique of current housing policy and present a possible, albeit tentative, alternative framework. Instead of one national housing policy, I have suggested that what is needed is as many housing policies as there are individuals and households that need them. What is required is a fundamental re-appraisal of the nature of housing policy and the processes it purports to control. Merely to replace a Modern Conservative government with a (New) Labour one would be only to alter the course of failure. The similarities in terms of the assumptions of government competence and responsibility far outweigh the ideological differences between the two parties. Likewise I could suggest that to replace a Democrat administration with a Republican one would be merely to tinker at the margins. Of course, to those who depend on current political systems these changes are all important. The impression is given that the Labour party merely need to be elected for a fundamental change to have occurred. It is as if the election of parties is an end in itself.

This position is undoubtedly symptomatic of the failure of public policy. It is based on a certainty that one particular position can be right. This certainty imbues this position with a moral significance that creates the imperative for its adoption. Thus national policies are characterised by a lack of alternatives. I have shown this particularly with the Modern Conservatives who have single-mindedly imposed a policy which purports to have choice and opportunity at its heart. The policy is predicated on a particular premise about what humans need and want, and because politicians "know" this they feel able to try and direct the lives of others.

I have suggested that this form of policy making is selfnegating and unsustainable. The Modern Conservatives can only maintain their policy of individual responsibility and independence by intervening in the markets which are supposed to be free of government intervention.

Likewise the post-war Labour government felt it necessary to place restrictions on private sector housing development in order to concentrate on public sector building (Malpass, 1990, Malpass & Murie, 1994), presumably again because they felt this is what people both needed and wanted. Thus they felt they could only provide what was wanted through the prohibition of the alternatives.

Both these examples could be seen to demonstrate government failure (although the experience of Modern Conservative government is a case of the failure of the notion of government failure!). The issue is not therefore one of choosing between different alternatives for central action, but of the rejection of this form of centralised policy making itself. The problem — the root cause of failure — is the belief that a universal notion of human need is ready to be found by those who know where to look. It is the belief that we have a particular nature that can be used as the determinant of government action. This predication operates as "common sense", and it is consequently not questioned as anything other than natural. The obvious problem, that different politicians and theorists offer fundamentally different and conflicting descriptions, is seemingly ignored. Whilst there is no universal agreement of what our nature is, there is a virtual consensus that there is such a thing as a universal human nature.

Thus, if this essay had been written in the 1970s, the same contradictions would have been evident. Indeed the work of Turner (1972, 1976) and Ward (1985) show that there was an awareness of this fundamental problem. It is therefore wrong to talk about the success or failure of housing policies (Barlow and Duncan, 1995). It is better to talk of gradations of failure and to seek to understand the causes of this failure. This essay has been an attempt to describe this failure and explain its provenance.

However, the descriptions presented in this essay have not been entirely negative. I have presented a description of human action and need that is anti-essentialist and incommensurable. This has not been presented as a version of reality, but as an anti-realist description that seeks to allow the complexity of individual "realities" to become manifest. Like Rorty (1989) I have rejected a realist or representationalist description of the world in the belief that our reality is defined as an internal process that is by no means necessarily commensurable with any other description. My description is thus unashamedly relativist.

This description suggests that a radical rethink of the purpose of housing policy is necessary. We need to recognise that a policy based on national imperatives is likely to fail. It is unlikely that incommensurable needs can be met by central government when it can never know what these needs are. This, of course, is a call for an intellectual and attitudinal change which recognises that the role of government can only be a limited one. Hence to counter the descriptions in this essay merely with the argument that it is more important to build or provide "homes" rather than to develop an alternative model or theory is itself a manifestation of the problem. We need to recognise that the provision of housing — which is turned into a home by the users — is not unproblematical. It is the manner that housing is provided and the consequent purpose that underpins them (which, of course, effects the nature of the output) that is the major issue. We thus need to rethink how housing is provided and, therefore, what it is meant to fulfil.

I have suggested that the basic dichotomy in housing policy is whether it is centrally or locally determined. Centrally determined, top-down policies have failed because they cannot be aware of the ends that individuals seek to fulfil through their dwelling. This can only be achieved through a framework that is under local control. By local, I mean the level which allows for individual participation and thus a level considerably smaller than the municipality. This does not make larger forms of political organisation redundant, but rather it is to suggest that they should be subservient to this lowest level. Instead of the current constitutional arrangements, where the only form of unlimited government is at national level, I am suggesting that all levels of government be limited, including self government.

Thus, as the title of this essay suggests, the necessary element for any sustainable housing policies are their limitation. National government must recognise the limits to its competence and thus restrict its actions to the areas of policy in which it can be effective. This is in the facilitating role of guaranteeing resources. Furthermore it should only be given those powers deemed necessary by lower levels of government. This process should continue until the community level which consists of individuals limited only by their own agreement. This agreed limitation is necessary only in so far as opportunities for self creation are equalised (Rorty, 1989).

These descriptions have implications for the role of housing discourse and research. I agree with Kemeny (1992b) that housing studies needs to become more reflexive. Yet this involves an appreciation of the epistemological function of discourse. Housing research should not merely mirror the assumptions of governmental competence. It should go beyond an analysis of the means and conditions of provision to look at the meaning that is attributed to the various levels in the housing process. The dominant concern with provision tends to suggest that housing is an end in itself, that is, that the size and nature of the housing stock is the issue. The concern of this essay has been to suggest that housing is a means and therefore what is important is what it does and not what it is.

This means a greater concern with the various levels of the process and how they may be integrated together rather than being seen as mutually exclusive and competing. Housing studies is becoming a more theoretically aware and sophisticated field of discourse and there is evidence of an increasing level of self-reflection (Gurney, 1991, Somerville, 1994). Yet there is still no attempt to suggest how the various levels and concerns of theorists can be linked together. The linkage, which is readily apparent, between the control of housing and the control of *my house* — between the individual control of space and the control of structures — has not been fully considered and is not fully understood. Such a project would need to bring together theoretical work on the home and the personal level with the work on local policy implementation and national provision and distribution. This is obviously a collective project drawing fully on the multi-disciplinary nature of the field.

This project is only a possibility if housing is considered not as a problem to be solved, but as a process that serves as the means to incommensurable ends. This implies that not only is housing not an end in itself, but neither is housing discourse. Therefore researchers need to consider the purposes that discourse is put to. It is all very well to suggest that housing studies needs to be more theoretically aware (Kemeny, 1992), but there is apparently no consideration of what it is to be made more theoretical for. We should not assume that theory necessarily adds to our understanding. Indeed it may do the opposite. As Shackle (1992) has suggested with regard to economics, it is easy to forget that a theory is merely a model with the aim of assisting explication and to see it instead as *the* picture of reality. As my description of the Modern Conservatives has shown, the consequences of confusing a theory — in this case of human nature — with "reality" and "truth" are far reaching. In this sense housing discourse has a significant role to play both in justifying the "reality" of the politicians, but also in deconstructing it.

This implies that housing studies should be concerned as much with method as with theory; with how researchers proceed within the field of discourse. Reflexivity is about the awareness of what we are doing and why. This has been recognised recently, particularly in the work of Somerville (1993, 1994). It is also one of the most important points I wish to press in this essay. I have presented a method entitled philosophical description, which I suggested is an attempt to bring together and use disparate and incommensurable ideas and notions. This is an open ended method that presupposes no outcome or closes off no area of possibility. It is not a theory, but a way of presenting ideas and placing them together to allow for a model to be put together, or for one to be pulled apart. It is a form of edifying philosophy (Rorty, 1981) where descriptions are presented as a form of dialogue. I am not seeking to persuade, but to engage others thinkers, writers and academics in a dialogue about the purpose of housing, about what it can achieve, and about what can be said about it. It offers no solutions or answers, merely a different way of asking the questions (Wittgenstein, 1953). It is a limited and limiting method — there are things which we cannot and would not want to say. This is, of course, as it should be. We should recognise what we can say and what we cannot.

We should be aware of what is the legitimate role for researchers and commentators, as well as for politicians and policy makers.

This limitation is only a problem for those seeking a total answer. It is my belief that a total answer is neither possible nor desirable. It may be that failure in policy and discourse is inevitable, but by accepting our limits we may restrict it to the level where perhaps some of our insights are still standing when the edifice crumbles.

BIBLIOGRAPHY

Adonis, A & Hames, T (1994) — *The Conservative Revolution?*, Manchester, Manchester University Press.

Albon, R & Stafford, D (1987) — *Rent Control*, London, Croom Helm.

Barlow, J & Duncan, S (1995) — *Success and Failure in Housing Provision: European Systems Compared*, Oxford, Pergamon.

Bauman, Z (1989) — *Modernity and the Holocaust*, Cambridge, Polity.

Bouman, Z (1991) — *Modernity and Ambivalence,* Cambridge, Polity.

Berlin, I (1969) — *Four Essays on Liberty*, Oxford, Oxford University Press.

Bhatti, M (1993) — *From Consumers to Prosumers: Housing for a Sustainable Future*, Housing Studies, Vol. 8, No. 2, pp. 98–108.

Birchall, J (1988) — *Building Communities: The Co-operative Way*, London, Routledge.

Boelhouwer, P & van der Heijden, H (1992) — *Housing Systems in Europe, Part 1: A Comparative Study of Housing Policy*, Delft, Delft University Press.

Boyson, R (1978) — *Centre Forward: A Radical Conservative Programme*, London, Temple Smith.

Burnett, J (1986) — *A Social History of Housing 1815–1985*, 2nd Edition, London, Methuen.

Clarke, J, Cochrane, A & Smart, C (1987) — *Ideologies of Welfare: From Dreams to Disillusion*, London, Hutchinson.

Cole, I & Furbey, R (1994) — *The Eclipse of Council Housing*, London, Routledge.

Coleman, A (1985) *Utopia on Trial: Vision and Reality in Planned Housing*, London, Hilary Shipman.

Coles, A (1992) — *Mortgage Rescue Schemes: An Overview*, Housing Review, Vol 41, No. 5.

Critchley, S (1992) — *The Ethics of Deconstruction: Derrida and Levinas*, Oxford, Blackwell.

Damer, S (1989) — *From Moorepark to 'Wine Alley': The Rise and Fall of a Glasgow Housing Scheme*, Edinburgh, Edinburgh University Press.

Daunton, M (1987) — *A Property Owning Democracy*, London, Faber.

Department of The Environment (1987) — *Housing: The Government's Proposals*, London, HMSO.

Department of the Environment (1995a) — *Provision of Social Housing — Background Analysis: Households in England, Their Tenure, and the Housing Stock, 1991–2001*, London, DOE.

Department of the Environment (1995b) — *Our Future Homes: Opportunity, Choice, Responsibility*, London, HMSO.

Depres, C (1991) — *The Meaning of Home; Literature Review and Directions for Future Research and Theoretical Development*, The Journal of Architectural and Planning Research, Vol. 8, No. 2, pp. 96–115.

Derrida, J (1976) — *Of Grammatology*, Baltimore, John Hopkins University, trans.

Derrida, J (1978) — *Writing and Difference*, London, Routledge, trans.

Derrida, J (1993) — *Aporias,* Stanford, Stanford University Press, trans.

Doyal, L & Gough, I (1991) — *A Theory of Human Need*, Basingstoke, MacMillan.

Dwelly, T (1992) — *Abandoned*, Roof, Vol. 17, No. 2.

Eatwell, J (1992) — *Britain Doesn't Need Another Housing Boom*, Observer, 23. 08. 92.

Eleftheriades, S (1992) — *The Engine of Recovery*, Housing, Vol. 28, No. 8.

Elshtain, J (1992) — *Don't Be Cruel: Reflections on Rortyian Liberalism*, in Conway, D & Seery, J — The Politics of Irony: Essays in Self Betrayal, New York, St. Martin's Press, pp. 197–217.

Eriksen, E (1950) — *Childhood and Society*, New York, Norton.

Eriksen, E (1968) — *Identity: Youth in Crisis*, London, Faber & Faber.

Ermish, J (Ed) (1990) — *Housing and the National Economy*, Aldershot, Avebury.

Forrest, R & Murie, A (1988) — *Selling the Welfare State: The Privatisation of Public Housing*, London, Routledge.

Foucault, M (1972) — *The Archaeology of Knowledge*, London, Routledge, trans.

Foucault, M (1977) — *Discipline and Punish: The Birth of the Prison*, London, Penguin, trans.

Foucault, M (1978) — *The History of Sexuality: Volume 1, Introduction*, London, Penguin, trans.

Foucault, M (1980) — *Power/ Knowledge: Selected Interviews and Other Writings, 1972–77*, London, Harvester, trans.

Foucault, M (1988) — *Technologies of the Self*, in Martin, L, Gutman, H and Hutton, P, pp. 16–49.

Gadamer, H–G (1975) — *Truth and Method*, London, Sheed and Ward, trans.

Gamble, A (1988) — *The Free Economy and the Strong State: The Politics of Thatcherism*, Basingstoke, MacMillan.

Giddens, A (1990) — *The Consequences of Modernity*, Cambridge, Polity.

Giddens, A (1991) — *Modernity and Self Identity: Self and Society in the Late Modern Age*, Cambridge, Polity.

Giddens, A (1994) — *Beyond Left and Right: The Future of Radical Politics*, Cambridge, Polity.

Goodchild, B (1991) — *Postmodernism and Design: A Guide to Design Theory*, Housing Studies, Vol. 6, No. 2, pp. 131–144.

Gray, J (1993) — *Beyond the New Right: Markets, Government and the Common Environment*, London, Routledge.

Gray, J (1995) — *Isaiah Berlin*, London, Harper Collins.

Green, D (1987) — *The New Right: The Counterrevolution in Political, Economic and Social Thought*, London, Wheatsheaf.

Gross, D (1992) — *The Past in Ruins: Tradition and the Critique of Modernity*, Amherst, University of Massachusetts Press.

Gurney, C (1990) — *The Meaning of Home in the Decade of Owner Occupation*, Bristol, SAUS.

Gurney, C (1991) — *Ontological Security, Home Ownership and the Meaning of Home: A Theoretical and Empirical Critique*, Paper delivered to conference: 'Beyond a Nation of Home Owners', Sheffield, 22.04.91.

Hall, D (1994) — *Richard Rorty: Prophet and Poet of the New Pragmatism*, Albany, State University of New York Press.

Harvey, D (1991) — *The Condition of Postmodernity*, Oxford, Blackwell.

Haworth, A (1994) — *Anti-libertarianism: Markets, Philosophy and Myth*, London, Routledge.

Hayek, F (1960) — *The Constitution of Liberty*, London, Routledge.

Hayek, F (1982) — *Law, Legislation and Liberty*, London, Routledge.

Hayek, F (1994) — *Hayek on Hayek: An Autobiographical Dialogue*, edited by Kresge, S and Wenar, L, London, Routledge.

Heidegger, M (1962) — *Being and Time*, Oxford, Blackwell, trans.

Heidegger, M (1993) — *Building Dwelling Thinking*, in Basic Writings, revised and expanded edition, edited by Krell, D, London, Routledge, pp. 343–364, trans.

Hills, J (1991) — *Unravelling Housing Finance: Subsidies, Benefits and Taxation*, Oxford, Clarendon.

Hindess, B (1987) — *Freedom, Equality and the Market: Arguments on Social Policy*, London, Tavistock.

Honderich, T (1990) — *Conservatism*, London, Hamish Hamilton.

Hughes, M (1992) — *Homes Slump Leaves 1.4m in Mortgage Trap*, Guardian, 12.11.92.

Hutton, W (1992) — *The Housing Market: How to Prevent Boom and Bust*, Housing Review, Vol. 41, No. 4.

Illich, I (1971) — *Deschooling Society*, London, Penguin.

Illich, I (1973) — *Tools for Conviviality*, London, Marion Boyars.

Illich, I (1992) — *In the Mirror of the Past: Lectures and Addresses 1978–1990*, London, Marion Boyars.

Illich, I et Al (1977) — *Disabling Professions*, London, Marion Boyars.

Illich, I & Sanders, B (1988) — *ABC: The Alphabetisation of the Popular Mind*, London, Penguin.

Jacobs, J (1961) — *The Death and Life of Great American Cities: The Failure of Town Planning*, London, Penguin.

Jencks, C (1989) — *What is Postmodernism?*, 3rd edition, London, Academy Editions.

Jordan, B (1987) — *Rethinking Welfare*, Oxford, Blackwell.

Jordan, B (1989) — *The Common Good: Citizenship, Morality and Self-Interest*, Oxford, Blackwell.

Kant, I (1990) — *Grounding for the Metaphysics of Morals*, in Cahn, S — Classics in Western Philosophy, 3rd edition, Indianapolis, Hackett, trans.

Kemeny, J (1992a) — *Housing and Social Structure: Towards a Sociology of Residence*, Bristol, SAUS.

Kemeny, J (1992b) — *Housing and Social Theory*, London, Routledge.

Kolb, D (1990) — *Postmodern Sophistications: Philosophy, Architecture and Tradition*, Chicago, University of Chicago Press.

Kukathas, C (1992) — *Freedom Versus Autonomy*, in Gray, J — The Moral Foundations of Market Institutions, London, IEA, pp. 101–114.

Langstaff, M (1988) — *Chosen to be Chosen*, Housing Review, Vol. 37, No. 5.

Le Corbusier (1927) — *Towards a New Architecture*, London, Butterworth, trans.

Le Courbusier (1929) — *The City of Tomorrow*, London, Butterworth, trans.

Le Grand, J & Robinson, R (1984) — *The Economics of Social Problems*, 2nd Edition, Basingstoke, MacMillan.

Levinas, E (1969) — *Totality and Infinity*, Dordrecht, Kluwer, trans.

Levitas, R (Ed) (1986a) — *The Ideology of the New Right*, Cambridge, Polity.

Levitas, R (1986b) — *Ideology and the New Right*, in Levitas, R (1986a).

Lindley, R (1986) — *Autonomy*, Basingstoke, MacMillan.

Loney, M (Ed) (1987) — *The State or the Market?: Politics and Welfare in Contemporary Britain*, London, Sage.

Lyotard, J–F (1984) — *The Postmodern Condition: A Report on Knowledge*, Manchester, Manchester University Press, trans.

MacPherson, C (Ed) (1978) — *Property: Mainstream and Critical Positions*, Oxford, Blackwell.

Malpass, P (1990) — *Reshaping Housing Policy: Subsidies, Rents and Residualisation*, London, Routledge.

Malpass, P & Murie, A (1994) — *Housing Policy and Practice*, 4th edition, Basingstoke, MacMillan.

Malpass, P & Means, R (Ed) (1993) — *Implementing Housing Policy*, Buckingham, Open University Press.

Malpass, P et Al (1993) — *Housing Policy in Action, Bristol*, SAUS.

Marquand, D (1988) — *The Paradoxes of Thatcherism*, in Skidelsky, R — Thatcherism.

Marshall, T (with Rees, R) (1985) — *Social Policy in the Twentieth Century*, London, Hutchinson.

Martin, L, Gutman, H & Hutton, P (1988) — *Technologies of the Self: A Seminar with Michel Foucault*, London, Tavistock.

Mathey, K (Ed) (1992) — *Beyond Self-Help Housing*, London, Mansell.

Minford P, Peel, M & Ashton, P (1987) — *The Housing Morass: Regulation, Immobility and Unemployment*, London, IEA.

Muellbauer, J (1990) — *The Great British Housing Disaster and Economic Policy*, London, IPPR.

Norberg-Schulz, C (1985) — *The Concept of Dwelling: On the Way to Figurative Architecture*, New York, Rizzoli.

Nozick, R (1974) — *Anarchy, State and Utopia*, Oxford, Blackwell.

Nozick, R (1981) — *Philosophical Explanations*, Oxford, Clarendon.

Ospina, J (1987) — *Housing Ourselves*, London, Hilary Shipman.

Oxley, M (1995) — *Private and social Rented Housing in Europe: Distinctions, Comparisons and Resource Allocation*, Scandinavian Housing and Planning Research, 12, pp. 59–72.

Page, D (1993) — *Building for Communities*, York, Joseph Rowntree Foundation.

Power, A (1987) — *Property Before People: The Management of Twentieth Century Council Housing*, Hemel Hempstead, Allen & Unwin.

Power, A (1993) — *Hovels to Highrise: State Housing in Europe Since 1850*, London, Routledge.

Priemus, H (1995) — *How to Abolish Social Housing?: The Dutch Case*, International Journal of Urban and Regional Research, Vol. 19, no. 1, pp. 145–155.

Ramirez, R et Al (1992) — *The Commodification of Self-Help Housing and State Intervention: Household Experiences in the Barrios of Caracas*, in Mathey K, 1992, pp. 95–144.

Rorty, R (1980) — *Philosphy and the Mirror of Nature*, Oxford, Blackwell.

Rorty, R (1989) — *Contingency, Irony and Solidarity*, Cambridge, Cambridge University Press.

Rorty, R (1991a) — *Objectivity, Relativism and Truth: Philosophical Papers, Vol 1*, Cambridge, Cambridge University Press.

Rorty, R (1991b) — *Essays on Heidegger and Others: Philosophical Papers, Vol 2*, Cambridge, Cambridge University Press.

Rose, R (1989) — *Ordinary People in Public Policy: A Behavioural Analysis*, London, Sage.

Ryan, A (1984) — *Property and Political Theory*, Oxford, Blackwell.

Ryan, A (1987) — *Property*, Buckingham, Open University Press.

Saunders, P (1990) — *A Nation of Home Owners*, London, Unwin Hyman.

Saunders, P & Williams, P (1988) — *The Constitution of the Home: Towards a Research Agenda*, Housing Studies, Vol. 3, No. 2, pp. 81–93.

Schon, D (1991) — *The Reflective Practitioner: How Professionals Think in Action*, Aldershot, Avebury.

Scruton, R (1980) — *The Meaning of Conservatism*, London, Penguin.

Scruton, R (1984) — *A Short History of Modern Philosphy*, London, Ark.

Shackle, G (1992) — *Epistemics and Economics: A Critique of Economic Doctrines*, London, Transaction.

Shand, A (1990) — *Free Market Morality: The Political Economy of the Austrian School*, London, Routledge.

Skidelsky, R (Ed) (1988) — *Thatcherism*, London, Chatto and Windus.

Skinner, R & Rodell, M (Ed) (1983) *People, Poverty and Shelter: Problems of Self-Help Housing in the Third World*, London, Methuen.

Somerville, P (1989) — *Home Sweet Home: A Critical Comment on Saunders and Williams,* Housing Studies, Vol. 4, No. 2, pp. 113–118.

Somerville, P (1993) — *The Construction of Home*, paper presented to European Network of Housing Research conference, Budapest, September, 1993.

Somerville, P (1994) — *On Explanations of Housing Policy*, Scandinavian Housing and Planning Research, 11, 211–230.

Spinelli, E (1989) — *The Interpreted World: An Introduction to Phenomenological Psychology*, London, Sage.

Spittles, D (1992) — *Mortgage Lifeline Runs into Arrears*, Observer Housing Report, 05.07.92.

Steiner, G (1978) — *Heidegger*, London, Fontana.

Taylor, C (1991) — *The Ethics of Authenticity*, Cambridge, Mass, Harvard University Press.

Toulmin, S (1990) — *Cosmopolis: The Hidden Agenda of Modernity*, Chicago, University of Chicago Press.

Turan, M (Ed) (1990) — *Vernacular Architecture: Paradigms of Environmental Response*, Aldershot, Avebury.

Turner, J (1972) — *Housing as a Verb*, in Turner & Fichter — *Freedom to Build.*

Turner, J (1976) — *Housing by People: Towards Autonomy in Building Environments*, London, Marion Boyars.

Turner, J & Fichter, R (Ed) (1972) — *Freedom to Build*, New York, MacMillan.

Uduku, O (1994) — *Tradition, Continuity and Change: The Urban Fabric of South Eastern Nigeria in the 1990s*, in Awotona, A — People, Place and Development, Newcastle, CARDO, pp. 662–671.

Van Zijl, V (1993) — *A Guide to Local Housing Needs Assessment*, Coventry, Chartered Institute of Housing.

Waldron, J (1988) — *The Right to Private Property*, Oxford, Clarendon.

Ward, C (1985) — *When We Build Again: Let's Have Housing That Works*, London, Pluto Press.

Ward, C (1990) — *Talking Houses*, London, Freedom Press.

Ward, C (1991) — *Influences: Voices of Creative Dissent*, Bideford, Green Books.

Watson, L & Harker, M (1993) — *Community Care Planning: A Model for Housing Need Assessment*, London, CIH/NFHA.

Weil, S (1987) — *The Need for Roots*, London, Ark, trans

Whitehead, C & Kleinman, M (1992) — *A Review of Housing Needs Assessment*, London, Housing Corporation.

Willets, D (1992) — *Modern Conservatism*, London, Penguin.

Wittgenstein, L (1953) — *Philosophical Investigations*, Oxford, Blackwell.

Wolff, J (1991) — *Robert Nozick: Property, Justice and the Minimal State*, Cambridge, Polity.

Index

Access 186, 191-3
Adam Smith Institute 77
Agency 39-41, 49, 175, 178, 185
  individual 133, 137,
  moral 145
  see also Individualism
Aggregates 33-8, 185
Authenticity 176-79
  see also Autonomy, Self creation
Anti-essentialism 56, 129, 135, 145
  see also Relativism
Autonomy 23, 142-48, 149-50,
  175-179
  see also Authenticity, Self
  creation, Self description

Baldwin, S 93
Basic trust 162
Bauman, Z 136, 142
Benefits
  means tested 192
  universal 192
Berlin, I 129-133, 142, 144, 148,
  164
Bhatti, M 189
Birchall, J 19, 52, 160
Boelhouwer, P 117-8
Boyson, R 74, 88, 94-5
Burke, E 93

Centre for Policy Studies 77
Citizenship 71-2, 85, 89-92, 96
Control of housing 158, 186,
  188-91
Critchley, S 58

Damer, S 39
Davidson, D 134
Depres, C 141

Derrida, J 25, 43, 58, 163
Disraeli, B 93
Doyal, L 143-4, 149-52
Dwelling, 15, 24, 113-4, 141,
  160-1, 161-74, 176
  implicit nature of 162
  political dimension of 167-70

Eatwell, J 105, 107
Effective choice 180-1
Elshtain, J 136
Epistemology 43
Ermish, J 98
Essentialism 49

Final vocabulary 134-5, 145, 148,
  162
  see also Rorty, R
Forrest, R 62, 73, 82, 115
Foucault, M 116-7, 163
Foundationalism 49, 148-9
Fulfilment of needs 35, 154-5, 158,
  188, 193, 196

Gadamer, H-G 163
Gamble, A 63, 74
Geddes, P 52
Giddens, A 123, 161
Goodchild, B 25
Goodman, P 52
Gough, I 143-4, 149-52
Gray, J 123, 129-33, 145
Green, D 88
Gross, D 163
Gurney, C 26, 37-8, 43, 140-1,
  159-60, 197

Habitual 162-3, 166, 167-8, 178,
  179

Harvey, D 20
Haworth, A 51-2, 131
Hayek, F 86, 92-3, 100-2, 128-9, 131, 180
Heath, E 93
Hegel, G 93
Heidegger, M 23, 160, 163, 176-77
    equipment 162, 178, 188
Heijden, H van der 117-8
Hindess, B 75-78
Home 140-1, 159-60, 197
Home ownership, *see* Owner occupation
Honderich, T 74, 80
Housing Act 1988 69
Housing Action Trusts 69
Housing associations 67-70, 105, 156
Housing Association Grant 67, 69
Housing Corporation 109, 112
Housing (Homeless Persons) Act 1977 95
Housing Investment Programmes 115
Housing market package 109-10, 113
Housing Revenue Accounts 70
Howard, E 52
Hutton, W 105

Ideology 37, 102-4
    Modern Conservative 74-79
    see also Modern Conservatives
Illich, I 28, 160, 165-70
Independent Rented Sector 67, 105
Individualism 81-2, 87-8, 104, 114, 132-3, 139-141
    see also Agency, Personal
Institute of Economic Affairs 77

Jacobs, J 169
Jencks, C 164
Jordan, B 72, 100, 103

Kant, I 130, 142
    Kantianism 80, 85-6, 102, 145
Kemeny, J 26, 41-49, 143-4, 197
Kleinman, M 155
Kohl, H 93
Kolb, D 50
Kukathas, C 144, 146

Le Corbusier 20-1, 24, 50
Levinas, E 25
Levitas, R 90-1, 98
Liberal ironism 133-5
    see also Rorty, R
Libertarianism 51-8, 127, 133-4, 135-8, 142
Limits 185-88, 196-7, 198-9
    defined 125-8
Lindley, R 142, 143
Local authorities 66, 68-70, 89, 116
Local Government and Housing Act 1989 70-1, 113
Local housing companies 113
Lyotard, J-F 21, 24, 40-1

Major, J 17, 34, 35, 37, 60
Marquand, D 94
Marx, K 93
Mathey, K 179
Merit goods 152, 157
Modern Conservatism 16, 17, 22, 58, 59-118, 121-3, 131, 132, 139-40, 147, 149, 150, 157, 160, 165, 179, 194-5, 198
    see also Ideology
Modernity 20, 22, 27, 50, 59-62, 114-8, 122-3, 126-7, 142, 158, 159, 163-4, 165-70, 185
Mortgage rescue schemes 108-9, 110
Muellbauer, J 98
Murie, A 62, 73, 82, 115

Needs 147-158, 192, 195
     lack of something 153-4
     necessity 153-5
Negative equity 106
Negative freedom 128-33
Non-patterned principle 56, 102,
     135, 146, 161
     see also Nozick, R
Norberg-Schulz, C 23, 160, 162,
     168,176
Nozick, R 51-58, 86, 89, 93, 102,
     128-9, 180
     coercive philosophy 53
     philosophical explanation 54-5, 57

Oakeshott, M 93
Ospina, J 52
Owner occupation 66, 69, 71, 72-3,
     104-14, 189, 192
Ownership 78-85
     see also Property, Property
     owning democracy
Oxley, M 118

Page, D 156
Perception 15, 36-7, 49,83, 152,
     156-7
Personal 22, 197
     Personalisation 25, 174
     see also Individualism
Philosophical description 57-8
Plato 92, 93
Pluralism 124, 132-3
Positive freedom 129-31
Postmodernity 24-5, 50-1, 164, 170
Power, A 17-9, 118, 169
Practical consciousness 161, 174
Priemus, H 117
Private landlords 66, 111
     rent control 67
Privatisation 96
Property 17, 71-114
     property rights 86, 89-91, 103
     see also Ownership

Property owning democracy 25, 36,
     71-3, 107, 111

Rationality 38, 40, 130-1, 142-6,
     150
Reagan, R 93
Relativism 148-9, 196
     see also Anti-essentialism
Right-to-Buy 35, 64, 67, 146-7,
     191
Rights 148
Roddell, M 179
Rorty, R 49, 50, 57, 133-7, 142,
     147, 148, 164, 185, 195
     edifying philosophy 198
Rose, R 103-4
Ryan, A 79, 91

Salisbury, Marquis of 93
Saunders, P 37, 46-7, 80-2, 97,
     140, 159
Scruton, R 74, 78-81, 84, 90, 94,
     96, 97, 100-2.
Security 23
Segal, W 52
Self creation 135-8, 146, 174-81,
     185, 186, 191, 197
     defined 176
     see also Authenticity, Autonomy
Self description 145, 177
     see also Autonomy
Shackle, G 40-1, 43, 198
Skidelsky, R 74
Skinner, R 179
Social democracy 75, 85, 89, 116,
     122, 143
Somerville, P 26, 37, 47, 57, 141,
     159-60, 197, 198
Standards 33-8, 171, 185, 186, 191

Taylor, C 123-4
Tenants Choice 69
Tenure apartheid 190-1

Thatcher 17, 34, 35, 36, 60,
  Thatcherism 74
Tradition 60-2, 84-5, 161-5, 166,
  179
Turner, J 19, 20, 52, 153, 160,
  171-74, 179, 186, 195
  existential significance 153, 173
  housing as a noun 22-3, 25, 173
  housing as a verb 22-3, 173
  oppressive house 171-2, 173
  supportive shack 171

Uduku, O 161, 169-70

Vernacular 165-66
Vernacular dwelling 165-74, 179-81

Waldron, J 79
Ward, C 19, 52, 195
Weil, S 39
White Paper 1987 65-71, 73, 87-8,
  90
White Paper 1995 112, 139
Whitehead, C 155
Willets, D 60-1
Williams, P 37, 46-7
Wittgenstein, L 134, 198
Woolf, J 52